TWENTIETH CENTURY INTERPRETATIONS
OF

THE RAPE
OF THE LOCK

A Collection of Critical Essays

Edited by

G. S. ROUSSEAU

Prentice-Hall, Inc. *Englewood Cliffs, N. J.*

A SPECTRUM BOOK

For Maynard Mack

PRENTICE-HALL INTERNATIONAL, INC. (*London*)
PRENTICE-HALL OF AUSTRALIA, PTY. LTD. (*Sydney*)
PRENTICE-HALL OF CANADA, LTD. (*Toronto*)
PRENTICE-HALL OF INDIA PRIVATE LTD. (*New Delhi*)
PRENTICE-HALL OF JAPAN, INC. (*Tokyo*)

Contents

Introduction

by G. S. Rousseau

Alexander Pope (1688–1744) has been described variously as "a Catholic and cripple" by some of his friends, as "the Wasp of Twickenham" by his enemies, and as "a spider" by himself. There is some but not very much truth to each of these appellations. He was the only child of elderly, Catholic parents (his father was a wealthy linen draper) and from the twelfth year of life he was deformed, eventually shrinking to a height of four feet, six inches.[1] A bachelor, he passed his days writing poetry and taking care of an invalid mother at his "Villa at Twickenham," as he himself called it, a small but splendid country house with spacious gardens, an extensive "prospect," and the most exquisitely adorned grotto in England. Ill health, coupled with his religion, limited his opportunities for leading an active life at court, in politics, and in town with his friends the Queen Anne "wits"—Addison, Arbuthnot, Berkeley, Gay, Steele, Swift—but he was no recluse or social pariah; he mixed with literary lights of the day and cultivated the "art of friendship" at every opportunity. He was indubitably the greatest poet of his generation, the literary lion of his age. Dr. Johnson was not asking a rhetorical question when he wrote, "If Pope be not a poet, where is poetry to be found?"[2]

Pope was also a prolific writer, especially if we consider the painstaking method of extensive revision by which he attained the perfection of his final products. By the age of nine or ten, he was writing verse and planning for future poems. His first published poems were *Pastorals*, which appeared in 1709 as part of Tonson's *Miscellany*. Soon after 1709 followed *An Essay on Criticism* (1711), which was praised by Addison in the *Spectator* and damned by Dennis; *The Rape of the Lock* (1712);[3] *Windsor Forest* (1713); an enlarged version

---

[1] Marjorie Hope Nicolson and G. S. Rousseau, *This Long Disease, My Life: Alexander Pope and the Sciences* (Princeton, 1968).

[2] G. B. Hill, ed., *Lives of the English Poets* (Oxford, 1905), III, 251.

[3] Contributors' preferences account for the different references to Pope's poem in this volume. Sometimes it appears as *The Rape of the Lock,* and sometimes as *Rape of the Lock.*

of *The Rape of the Lock* (1714); and translations of Homer's *Iliad*
(1715–20). His middle period includes translations of the *Odyssey*
(1725–26), written with the help of Broome and Fenton, *The Dunciad*
(1728) in three books, and several volumes of *Miscellanies,* composed
in collaboration with Swift. By the early 1730's Pope had "stoop'd to
Truth and moraliz'd his *Song,*" for his verse was now less descriptive
and fictive, and was concerned instead with morality and the exposure
of vice, corruption, and dullness. All the works of his late years attest
a profound interest in reforming taste and sensibility: *Moral Essays*
(1731–34), *Imitations of Horace* (1733–38), *An Essay on Man* (1733–34),
and the last poem of his life, the revised *Dunciad* (1743) in four books
with Colley Cibber, the Poet Laureate, enthroned in the place of
Lewis Theobald. Despite irritability and occasional meanness, Pope
was liked, even appreciated, by friends and critics. Swift realized what
a consummate poet he was, Gay adored him, and Dr. Johnson held
that he had carried versification in the eighteenth-century couplet
mode as far as it could go: "New sentiments and new images others
may produce, but to attempt any further improvement of versification
will be dangerous. Art and diligence have done their best, and what
shall be added will be the effort of tedious toil and needless curiosity." [4]

I

Pope told Joseph Spence, his Boswell, that he started to write "an
epic poem when about twelve." [5] What his work would have been
like if completed we shall never know, but it probably was nothing
like his other "heroick poem," *The Rape of the Lock*. His translations
of Homer and *The Dunciad* aside, Pope's *Rape of the Lock* is the
only "epic poem" he ever wrote, mock-epic though it is. The immediate stimulus for its composition was a real event among real friends
of Pope. Sometime late in 1711 or early in 1712, a lock of the hair of
Miss Arabella Fermor, the daughter of a prominent Catholic family,
had been cut off by Lord Petre. Whether it was cut in jest or seriously,
the young Arabella was upset, the Fermors and Petres fell out, and
John Caryll, a friend of both, solicited Pope to reconcile the families
by writing verses. Pope did, and the poem had the desired effect. More
important for poetry, however, he composed a perfect little poem in
two cantos, but he was unsatisfied and saw that he could improve it

---

[4] Hill, *op. cit.,* III, 251.

[5] James M. Osborn, ed., *Observations, Anecdotes, and Characters of Books* (Oxford,
1966), I, 16.

further by the addition of sylph machinery. He completed his new five-canto *Rape of the Lock* within two years, writing what Dr. Johnson later called "the most airy, the most ingenious, and the most delightful of all his compositions." [6]

Although Pope's mixture of sylph machinery and epic action was new—he himself considered it the most successful product of his poetic craft—the mock-epic form in which he wrote *The Rape of the Lock* was not. The Restoration had given rise to many forms of satire, ranging from "low" brawling burlesque in *Hudibras* (1663–78) to Dryden's "high" heroic wit in *Absalom and Achitophel* (1681–82). Dr. Ian Jack has written that although *Hudibras* is "low satire" and *MacFlecknoe* is merely "mock-heroic," *The Rape of the Lock* is a "complex mock-heroic." [7] Pope's urbane satire represents the culmination of a tradition of pseudo-epic poems in which the values and idiosyncrasies of an entire culture are satirized. Whereas society in the Restoration tended toward libertinism and profligacy, in the age of Queen Anne (1702–14) it became more refined, perhaps artificially so. Great families and patrons of the arts gathered at court, sheltered from the outside world and devoted to the pursuit of their personal interests.[8] The shift from libertinism to restraint in aristocratic manners is reflected in *The Rape of the Lock* where "at every Word, a Reputation dies." Calculated elegance became a dominant characteristic of the upper classes. Leonard Woolf, the husband of Virginia, wrote in his autobiography that if "you want to know what a particular period was like, the nature of its society and classes, the kind of people who lived in it, you can learn this from the way in which the people met and entertained one another formally." [9] Pope would have agreed with this sentiment, for he satirized, mildly and genially, the restrained and refined manners of the upper classes by sending Belinda to a fashionable party at Hampton Court, where ministers of state do "sometimes Counsel take—and sometimes *Tea*."

The tradition of mock-epic poems in which Pope wrote does not detract from the novelty of his "invention"; on the contrary, it was precisely this tradition, its conventions and "rules," that permitted him to innovate, to deviate in part from the conventions of the form, and to create his own allusive mock-epic. His satire is cast in the form of a palpably credible plot in which the various characters (Sir

[6] *Life of Pope*, III, 101.

[7] *Augustan Satire: Intention and Idiom in English Poetry 1660–1750* (Oxford, 1952).

[8] James Sutherland, "Poetry in a Polite Society," in *Preface to Eighteenth Century Poetry* (Oxford, 1948).

[9] *Downhill All the Way* (New York, 1967), p. 103.

Plume, the Baron, Belinda) make themselves appear ridiculous by their thought, speech, and actions. Pope innovated in a number of ways. While he adhered to contemporary critical thought regarding the necessity of "fable" and its accompanying actions in epic poetry,[10] he deviated from Dryden's mock epics by epic amplitude (Pope's five-part structure is more extensive than any of Dryden's structures), and by parodying classical deities as minuscule (and allegorical) Rosicrucian sylphs. The sylphs are of particular interest insofar as they illustrate Pope's epic reversal. Although they profess to guard Belinda, they are thoroughly inconsequential—protective nothings.

Another aspect of Pope's "invention" is the perfected heroic couplet; no other poet except Shakespeare ever reaped such rich returns from his literary medium. Sustained heroic couplets (i.e., closed, iambic pentameter couplets with a decided caesura placed near the middle of the line) require that two lines serve something of the function of a stanza. Frequently the relation between the first and second line, or between the halves of a single line, is one of antithesis. Pope wrote *The Rape of the Lock* in heroic couplets because he wished to emphasize by strong contrast or opposition antithetic aspects of the truly "epic" world and Belinda's pretentious world of petty social values. Additionally, Pope's couplets are capable of achieving every known type of poetic effect, including high seriousness and low comedy, optimism and gloom, mirth and despair, and a host of other "atmospheres" or poetic states. The narrator of the poem "soars and sinks," [11] magnifies and diminishes his characters, reaches towering climaxes, and descends to abysmal depths. Such control of external form is part of Pope's technical virtuosity.

Sound, too, is an aspect of verse that Pope emphasizes: "the *Sound* must seem an echo to the *Sense*," he had written in *An Essay on Criticism,* and he adhered to this critical precept in *The Rape of the Lock.* For example, in the lines describing Belinda's "toyshop of the Heart," repetitions of sound collaborate with quick changes of syntax to suggest the crammed clutter and unceasing obsolescences that characterize Belinda's inner life:

> Where Wigs with Wigs, with Sword-Knots Sword-Knots strive,
> Beaus banish Beaus, and Coaches Coaches drive (I, 101–102)

Pope's other stylistic devices include balance and parallelism, antithesis, juxtaposition, zeugma, and chiasmus. Masterful use of balance

---

[10] *Monsieur Bossu's Treatise of the Epick Poem, Translated by* "*W.J.*" (London, 1695), which influenced Pope considerably.

[11] See Edna Leeke Steeves, *The Art of Sinking in Poetry, Martin Scriblerus' Peri Bathous* (New York, 1952).

and parallelism occurs in the description of Belinda at the opening of Canto III:

> On her white Breast a sparkling *Cross* she wore,
> Which *Jews* might kiss, and Infidels adore. (7–8)

Belinda's "Breast" is balanced by "Cross," the latter receiving from the former a startling accession of power to convert, and both together, perhaps, suggesting to the imagination a world so immaculate and shining that all other worlds pay it homage. Frequently, Pope's antitheses function in this same way—for example in the lines in the same passage describing Belinda's "smiles":

> Favours to none, to all she smiles extends,
> Oft she rejects, but never once offends. (11–12)

Here everything is contrasted with everything: Belinda's "Favours" with her "smiles," which are not at all comparable and which operate in totally different spheres; "none" and "all," in the sense that they are equally objects of her unmitigated detachment; even the temporal terms "oft" and "never," defining the bounds of her rejections and offences. Equally surprising effects result from Pope's juxtapositions, which allow the distinguishing reader an insight into Belinda's elegant world. "Puffs, Powders, Patches, Bibles, Billet-doux" (I, 138) is perhaps the single best description in the poem of the confusions of that world, epitomized in Belinda's untidy dressing-table. Parodying Milton's description of chaos—"Rocks, Caves, Fens, Bogs, Dens, and shades of death"—Pope's line vividly shows us the failure of elegance to sort out its values.

A special form of juxtaposition that Pope often uses to convey a like sense of incongruity is zeugma, of which an oft-quoted example occurs at the climax of the passage describing Hampton Court:

> Here Thou, Great *Anna!* whom three Realms obey,
> Dost sometimes Counsel take—and sometimes *Tea.*

Even Queen Anne, who kept up the ancient claim of the English crown to rule France as well as Britain and Ireland, is human. She must take time out for coffee as well as strategies of state, and (so the zeugma hints) values one about equally with the other. Professor William Frost is right when he says that in *The Rape of the Lock,* "every poetic and logical energy is brought into focus, no syllable giving the effect of having been placed or selected at random." [12] If

[12] "*The Rape of the Lock* and Pope's Homer," *Philological Quarterly,* VIII (1947), 328.

"*Sound* and *Sense*" are wedded, so, too, is the relation of "rhyme and reason." Pope also infuses his poem with a certain *je ne sais quoi,* "a grace beyond the reach of Art," as he called this aesthetic effect in the *Essay on Criticism.* No one can mistake Pope's couplets in *The Rape of the Lock* for those of his predecessors in the Restoration—Cowley, Oldham, Rochester, or Dryden.[13]

II

Although the realism of *The Rape of the Lock* differs in tone and quality from that of Defoe's *Moll Flanders* or Hogarth's engravings in *A Rake's Progress,* it nevertheless captures significant details of the world it delineates. Its satire on aristocratic manners makes a comment on polite society at large, on fashionable women in particular, which exposes all values, especially trifling and artificial ones, by exhibiting how small any world commensurate with them would have to be. Pope composed with a long tradition of satires on women in mind. Belinda at her dressing-table is the heiress of a whole race of previous lady charmers, from the playhouse girl in Restoration comedy to the cold coquette in fashionable London society. To an even greater degree than her predecessors, Belinda moves in a filigree world, a "fairyland" adorned with jewels, china, lap-dogs, and snuff-boxes. She is the tantalizing heroine who, like Narcissa in *Moral Essay II: Of the Characters of Women,* eventually must come under the censure of the honest rebuker, the narrator himself. Addison and Steele had written a good deal on women in the *Spectator,* and it is partly in the light of their views that Pope's poem should be considered. "How much nobler," Steele wrote of fashionable ladies in *Spectator 33,* "is the Contemplation of *Beauty* heightened by *Virtue.*" Addison in *Spectator 81* voiced a similar opinion in noting that although "our English Women excell those of all Nations in *Beauty,* they should endeavour to outshine them in all other Accomplishments proper to the Sex." Belinda's "sacred Rites of Pride" are not what Addison had in mind as "Accomplishments proper to the Sex."

Although Pope remarked in his *Epistle to a Lady* that women are ruled by two passions only,

> Those, only fix'd, they first or last obey,
> The Love of Pleasure, and the Love of Sway,

[13] See Ruth Wallerstein, "The Development of the Heroic Couplet," *Publications of the Modern Language Association,* L (1935), 166–209.

he created in Belinda a heroine whose passions transcend "Pleasure" and "Sway." Her movements are seen to correspond to the glorious and bright light of "Sol," the pervasive supernatural divinity of the poem. Indeed "Belinda" herself is a sort of goddess and as such is truly "divine":[14] "Belinda smiled and all the World was gay." Despite her vanity, she is the only character in the poem capable of assuaging the fiercest of enemies:

> If to her share some Female Errors fall,
> Look on her Face, and you'll forget 'em all. (III, 17–18)

And although she is the butt of Pope's satire exposing the petulancy and insincerity of the fashionable game of love, she is also the romantic heroine, twice removed from her predecessors in Restoration comedy and poetic satire by virtue of her greater elegance and charm, and because of Pope's own fond attitude towards her. Rachel Trickett has aptly noted that a "deliberate ambiguity surrounds the heroine, the setting, and the situation itself." [15] The ambiguity of romantic affection and moral censure on the narrator's part is deliberate and derives in part from the poet's mood of light-hearted geniality and in part from the imagery of a glamorous world of coquettes and sylphs. Love, admiration, and regret are ingeniously woven into the fabric of the poem to a much greater degree than was customary in mock-heroic satire. Pope's later sterner moods—as, for example, in the *Moral Essays*—are here counteracted by a smiling benignity that he was never again to achieve in his writing career. It is doubtful that he could have effected this ingratiating mood without the help of the sylph imagery, the "light *Militia* of the Sky," and he knew that if the sylphs were to be included at all they had to be fully integrated into the "heroic" world. This meant endowing them with attributes—many times diminished, and therefore charming rather than disquieting—of the heathen ancient gods.

One critic has called all Pope's poetry "the poetry of allusion." [16] The title itself is allusive, "rape" deriving from the Latin word *rapere*, "to snatch"—more particularly, "to ravish" in the sense of epic plunder. Belinda's "lock" alludes to Martial's epigram ("I was loath, Belinda, to violate your lock; but I am pleased to have granted that much to your prayers," XII, 86) and Berenice's deified hairs. Allusion is used

---

[14] Belinda's divinity is discussed by Cleanth Brooks in "The Case of Miss Arabella Fermor," *The Well Wrought Urn*, included among the selections in this volume.
[15] *The Honest Muse* (Oxford, 1967), p. 167.
[16] Reuben A. Brower, *Alexander Pope: The Poetry of Allusion* (Oxford, 1959).

more generally in *small* sylphs parodying *large* epic deities and in the
verbal sense of individual lines recalling passages in classical Greek
and Latin poetry. Pope contributes to and makes innovations on the
usual forms of allusive poetry by recalling contexts as well as passages.[17] For example, he suggests Belinda's true state at the beginning
of Canto IV, after she has won at the game of ombre and has been
"raped" of her lock:

> But anxious Cares the pensive Nymph opprest,
> And secret Passions labour'd in her Breast;

These lines repeat the opening of the fourth *Aeneid*: "But the
queen (i.e., Dido), long since wounded by anxious cares . . . is torn
by secret passion." The parallel is exact, the meaning of Pope's allusion clear. But it has not been so apparent that, just as Dido's worries
are contrasted in Virgil with Aeneas' glib indifference at the end of
Book III, so are Belinda's cares contrasted with the Baron's exulta-
tions over his booty at the end of Canto III. The irony of the allusion
is that Dido's sexuality is totally different from Belinda's and yet *both*
women experience some reluctance in desire; *both* experience in their
outrage an intense passion hidden from their conscious minds. When
reading *The Rape of the Lock*, we must always remember that while
Pope was composing it he was daily reading and translating Homer's
Iliad and, although the "heroic" world of the *Iliad* is at odds with the
polite world of *The Rape of the Lock,* there is more similarity than
difference in the poetic spirit that unites them. The poet who writes,
following Homer, of "the wrath of Achilles" is also the poet who
writes of Belinda's "wrath" that "Hairs . . . less in sight" were not
chosen for the Baron's exploit; one consciousness mediates knowingly
and gracefully between the two worlds. Professor Maynard Mack has
commented on the importance of Pope's Homeric experience in in-
terpreting *The Rape of the Lock*: "What is clear is that Hera's
cestus, as Pope interprets it [in *Iliad* XIV], belongs to the same world
of discourse as Belinda, her Cross, and her Lock; and that either
Homer's erotic set piece has affected Pope's image of Belinda, or the
image of Belinda has affected his Homer, or both." [18] We may never
know which way Pope went. The important point is that the Homeric
world (particularly) as well as the epic world (generally) pervade
The Rape of the Lock from beginning to end, and that this inclusive-

[17] See Earl Wasserman, "The Limits of Allusion in *The Rape of the Lock*," included among the selections in this volume.
[18] Introduction to *Pope's Translations of Homer: The Twickenham Edition* (London, 1967) , VII, 245.

ness is nowhere more apparent than in the sylph machinery, although this machinery has been refined several grades by Pope, by a Christianizing element, by Miltonic parody (from *Paradise Lost*), and by epic diminution and aggrandizement, some of which results from the subtle use of and reference to two recent discoveries—the telescope and microscope—that opened up new worlds of "the small" and "the large" to Pope and his contemporaries.

If Pope treads a delicate balance between romantic celebration and moral censure, he also resolves the seeming antinomy they represent. Without using the jargon of Freudian psychological criticism or the discoveries of recent cultural anthropology, one can judiciously say that his resolution takes the form of the ultimate subject of the poem, "the true character of a lady." Belinda is not a true lady. If she were, she would not act as she does over a clip of her lock or exercise her spleen to such a vigorous degree in Pope's imaginative "Cave of Spleen." She lacks the knowledge of the common fate of coquettes like herself, "a *fop* their passion, but their prize a *sot*" (*Moral Essays* II, 247–48). But neither is Clarissa the "true lady." She lacks Belinda's feminine divinity and sparkling manner, and deals out moral precepts, however sound, with the righteous indignation of an English governess:

> Oh! if to dance all Night, and dress all Day,
> Charm'd the Small-pox, or chas'd old Age away;
> Who would not scorn what Huswife's Cares produce,
> Or who would learn one earthly Thing of Use?
> To patch, nay ogle, might become a Saint,
> Nor would it sure be such a Sin to paint.
> But since, alas! frail Beauty must decay,
> Curl'd or uncurl'd, since Locks will turn to grey,
> Since painted, or not painted, all shall fade,
> And she who scorns a Man must die a Maid;
> What then remains, but well our Pow'r to use,
> And keep good Humour still whate'er we lose? (V, 19–30)

This speech, which parodies that of Sarpedon to Glaucus in *Iliad XII*, illustrates that Clarissa is moral and heroic in an almost pedestrian manner. And yet, one should not depreciate her too far, like Thalestris (herself a far more unreliable figure), who calls her prude. Although Clarissa stands to lose whenever compared with Belinda, there is much in her advice that indicates that she is neither sexless nor asensual. Her delivery of the scissors, that "Fatal Engine," to the Baron may be seen as catty, the act of an older woman who secretly enjoys the blow to a young beauty's vanity; or it may be seen as the surgical and kindly meant intervention of one who clearly knows that the lock and all it symbolizes must go if Belinda is ever to grow up.

It is not possible to assess Clarissa's motives beyond this since the poem does not tell us enough to do so. How far Pope ultimately agrees with her is an insoluble question, but one thing is clear: however minor a character she may be and however subsidiary her role in the action, the poet has nevertheless given her an unusually long and effective speech at a crucial point in the action. If she is not the final word, her contribution is no less important for its not being absolute and ultimate. She is one of those elusive characters in poetry whose motives and remarks contain an element of paradox, and in this case we must attribute much of the responsibility for our bafflement to Pope himself, who has not given us any clue to Clarissa's character. Her keen sense of priorities reinforces his own attitude toward the bright world of "Sol" and she also serves as a foil to the poem's glittering "toyshop." To Belinda, on the other hand, Pope promises immortality; Belinda triumphs over time by her beauty. The ideal woman must be more than the embodiment of school-text morality, and it is this imaginary but never explicitly defined "lady" who never loses her temper, who always maintains a degree of levity however "dire her strait," and, most important, who realizes that she must submit to man in marriage and surrender her coquetry, if for no other reason than because "frail Beauty must decay"—it is this lady about whom Pope writes. His poem makes it evident that the ideal woman must possess a certain divinity within herself.

The Rape of the Lock is the work of a young man, and is understandably exuberant and lusty in its tone. It is also the genial poetry of a man who had warm and imaginative sympathy with romantic passions that life unequivocally thwarted. No one knew better than "the little Alexander the women laugh at" how to infuse his love poetry with the charms of a heroine whose feminine disposition was irresistible. Had Pope been satisfied merely to write a moral satire on the theme of "the vanity of refusing marriage," *The Rape of the Lock* would be a very different poem from what it is. It would be far less appealing as poetry because of its single-minded morality. Pope once remarked to Spence that no poem was worth writing unless it contained a moral, and he added that even in amatory verse, "the moral may be flung in by the way." [19] We know that Pope was too exacting a poet to fling in anything by the way and that his morality

---

[19] Osborn, *op. cit.*, I, 196.

is finely interwoven into the mock-heroic structure of the poem itself. If there is a morality here that can be briefly described, it is that in the world of Pope's poem the perfect woman is a hybrid of Belinda and Clarissa. Call her "Clarinda" if you will.

III

We can only guess at the effect of Pope's poem upon his contemporaries. It probably had a wholly pleasing effect on the eighteenth-century reader. Regarding its reception by individuals of high station, we can be more specific. Arabella Fermor, the "heroine" in real life, liked it so much that in 1714 she deliberately chose to have her name set in front of the poem. Shortly after 1714, she commissioned her portrait to be drawn, and is shown wearing the "sparkling *Cross*" mentioned in the poem (II, 7), obviously delighted that Pope had ascribed to her the attractiveness of a great beauty:[20]

> Not all the Tresses that fair Head can boast
> Shall draw such Envy as the Lock you lost. (V, 143–44)

Almost from the day of publication of the expanded version—March 2, 1714—the poem sold well. By March 12, Pope wrote to John Caryll, who had commissioned the work, that *The Rape of the Lock* "has in four days time sold to the number of three thousand." [21] By July, Pope placed the sales at well above six thousand, a tremendous number of sold copies for a poem at that time. I would not mention these figures if they did not indicate the popularity of the poem among London literati. Although this mock-epic was written as coterie poetry with a limited and particular aristocratic audience in mind, it has universal appeal that has sustained its popularity for more than two centuries.

Pope himself wrote an anonymous burlesque on *The Rape of the Lock,* which he called *A Key to the Lock, Or a Treatise proving, beyond all Contradiction, the dangerous Tendency of a late Poem entituled The Rape of the Lock, to Government and Religion, by Esdras Barnivelt.*[22] In his *Key,* a practical moral as well as harmful political

[20] Geoffrey Tillotson, ed., *The Rape of the Lock: The Twickenham Edition* (London, 1962), p. 98.

[21] George Sherburn, ed., *The Correspondence of Alexander Pope* (Oxford, 1956), I, 234.

[22] Published in 1715 and discussed by Norman Ault, *Prose Works of Alexander Pope* (Oxford, 1936).

significance is ascribed to the poem. Written in epic manner with allegorical characters, the work jestfully equates Belinda with Great Britain, the Baron with the Earl of Oxford, who at the time of the poem headed Queen Anne's government, Clarissa with Lady Masham, and Thalestris with the Duchess of Marlborough (both Lady Masham and the Duchess had political influence because of the Queen's attachment to them, and were rivals for her favor). Some of Pope's contemporaries found *The Rape of the Lock* immoral and distasteful, lacking in the true qualities of wit and judgment. John Dennis, a poet, dramatist, and critic, wrote *Remarks on Mr. Pope's Rape of the Lock* (1728), in which he severely attacked the poem for deviating from the rules of epic and for dealing in "trifles without morals." Dennis, who had previously criticized the *Essay on Criticism,* failed to understand that Pope's poem was well-designed for its own limited ends, that it was a mock-epic and not grand epic, that any new "invention"—indeed any imaginative poem—must to some extent modify the rules, especially when the poem in question is extensive. Dennis also charged Pope with not following conventional morality in epic as found in Boileau's *Le Lutrin,*[23] one of the first modern poems to mock epic form by ingenious means. Pope answered by inscribing the words "Clarissa's Speech" in his copy of Dennis' *Remarks* over Dennis' phrase "Clergy and Religion" as the object of Boileau's attack in *Le Lutrin.*[24] Few of Pope's contemporaries were as wrongheaded about the morality of *The Rape of the Lock* as was Dennis. Most of them realized that Clarissa's speech introduced the fixed norm of the poem, and that, despite the woman's unattractive qualities, the speech Pope gives her is, within its limits, unanswerable. This is not to minimize Pope's delight in creating Belinda, or to detract from her sensual charms; it is merely to demonstrate that Pope was indeed following the conventions of contemporary mock-epic by including a "moral" in his poem while innovating in the creation of two female characters, one important, the other minor, who stand in opposition to each other. Dr. Johnson appears to have understood this perfectly well when commenting on Pope's moral superiority to Boileau:

> The purpose of the Poet is, as he [Pope] tells us, to laugh at "the little unguarded follies of the female sex." It is therefore without justice that Dennis charges *The Rape of the Lock* with the want of a moral, and for that reason sets it below *The Lutrin,* which exposes the pride and discord of the clergy. Perhaps neither Pope nor Boileau has made the

[23] E. N. Hooker, ed., *Dennis,* II, 142–43.
[24] See the Tillotson edition of *The Rape of the Lock,* p. 394 and Appendix D.

world much better than he found it; but if they had both succeeded, it were easy to tell who would have deserved most from publick gratitude. The freaks, and humours, and spleen, and vanity of women, as they embroil families in discord and fill houses with disquiet, do more to obstruct the happiness of life in a year than the ambition of the clergy in many centuries. It has been well observed that the misery of man proceeds not from any single crush of overwhelming evil, but from small vexations continually repeated.[25]

The later history of the poem is one of acclaim and appreciation. Commended for its refined wit and imagination, Pope's poem delighted critics for the next two centuries by its charm and ironic play on aspects of the *beau monde*. Aaron Hill wrote the following words, only ten years after publication, in the middle of a rhapsody touched off by the thought of Pope's writing Dryden's epitaph:[26]

When my *Passions* feel his *Force*, I attend him [Pope] thro' the *Depths* of *Nature*, with the Reverence which is due to God-like *Wisdom* and *Philosophy*! And, while my Fancy flames, and glitters, in the Sportive Vastness of his *Levity*, where *Belinda's Hair* attracts him, I am transported at his *Wit*, and *Gaiety*, and grow *in Love* with Good *Breeding*!

Such delight was typical of the day; authors from Fielding to Dr. Johnson, from Addison to Goldsmith, were captivated by the poetic texture of the poem, its "rich brocade." Hazlitt delighted in reading it, although he knew not "whether to laugh or weep." One need only look at Aubrey Beardsley's renowned illustrations of *The Rape of the Lock*[27] to comprehend how the poem continued to enthrall the imagination of its readers in the nineteenth century and later.

Regardless of the name given it—whether it be called complex mock-epic, or, as Reuben Brower has called it, taking his cue from an eighteenth-century musical form, "a literary and social divertimento" —*The Rape of the Lock* is the finest example of witty mock-epic ever written. It continues to charm modern readers by its deft combination of the serious and the nonserious, both convincingly important in the fashionable world of a young London poet, "the gayest valetudinaire alive." It is ultimately a personal rather than public poem, one whose greatest achievement may well be the invention of the sylphs, those creatures of marvelousness who lend the poem tones of

[25] Hill, *op. cit.*, III, 234.
[26] *Plain Dealer*, No. 68, November 13, 1724.
[27] See his edition of 1898 and Stanley Weintraub, *Aubrey Beardsley* (New York, 1967).

lightness and delicacy unique in English poetry. Its burlesque mockery of supposedly pernicious aspects of high society is never altogether serious. And it is precisely this ability to imply without pointing a finger, to allude ever so lightly without clearly referring, that happily makes it contemporary for all times.

PART ONE

Interpretations

Introductory

by J. S. Cunningham

The ant's a centaur in his dragon world.
Pull down thy vanity, it is not man
Made courage, or made order, or made grace,
Pull down thy vanity, I say pull down.

Ezra Pound, The Pisan Cantos

"A poem on a slight subject requires the greatest care to make it considerable enough to be read." When Pope made this remark to his friend Joseph Spence, he had (it seems) *The Dunciad* chiefly in mind; and recent criticism of that poem has dwelt on the meticulous and often furtive care with which Pope, while apparently preoccupied with the ephemera, the sweepings and nonentities of Grub Street and Fleet Ditch, attempts to persuade us of their paradoxical importance as symptoms of a widespread, perhaps irretrievable decline in civilised standards. The dunces act out their grossly comic *charade* on a stage which reverberates with mutilated hints, distorted echoes, of very "considerable" things—classical epic, the Scriptures, Milton. As embodiments of the reductive will, defacers of the ideals these echoes call to mind, the dunces attain in the poem an unenviable significance far beyond their mere status in Pope's London. Conversely, as the posturing mimics of nobler figures, they are dwarfed by their own pretensions. This double activity of inflation and deflation, through which the dunces are at once below consideration *and* a serious menace, Pope achieves in so far as he contrives to expose the trivial by insinuation, allusion and parody—in so far as he "implies and projects the possible other case, the case rich and edifying where the actuality is pretentious and vain." [1]

"Slight is the subject." This admission is made in the opening paragraph of *The Rape of the Lock,* and of course the poem is concerned— though not merely, nor simply—with a trivial episode. Lord Petre had snipped off a lock of Miss Arabella Fermor's hair, causing ill-feeling between their families. They had already, as it were, anticipated Pope by taking an amorous prank with extravagant seriousness. Pope outdoes them in absurdity, giving the incident full epic treatment. In other words, classical epic provides the "rich and edifying" contrast against which the vanity and pretentiousness of the *beau monde* can be judged.

Even the admission of the triviality of the poem's "subject"—

> Slight is the Subject, but not so the Praise,
> If She inspire, and He approve my Lays—

carries unsuspected weight: it echoes closely, and scales down, two lines from Virgil's fourth *Georgic,* which was itself much commended in Pope's time as the classical example of making mundane material "considerable enough" by means of dignified treatment. Pope recalled Virgil's poem again in writing his Postscript to the translation of *The Odyssey.* His remarks fit *The Rape of the Lock* very neatly:

> Laughter implies censure; inanimate and irrational beings are not objects of censure; therefore these may be elevated as much as you please, and no ridicule follows, but when rational beings are represented above their real character, it becomes ridiculous in Art, as it is vicious in Morality. The *Bees* in *Virgil,* were they rational beings, would be ridiculous in having their actions and manners represented on a level with creatures so superior as men; since it would imply folly or pride, which are the proper objects of Ridicule.[2]

Belinda at the dressing-table's "sacred Rites," the Baron building his altar of "twelve vast *French* Romances," are caught in attitudes of comic seriousness. Representing them, as indeed they conceive of themselves, "above their real character," coquette as goddess, philanderer as hero, the poem matches their moral failings with artistic absurdity.

The discrepancy between the world of heroic passions and conflicts,

[1] Henry James, "The Lesson of the Master." A fuller quotation is given on p. 59 [of Cunningham's book]. An outstanding recent discussion of *The Dunciad* is Aubrey Williams, *Pope's "Dunciad": A Study of its Meaning,* Methuen, 1955.

[2] *Odyssey,* V, 299–300.

on the one hand, and the microcosm of modish *amours* and scandal, on the other, is firmly adumbrated from the start:

> What dire Offence from am'rous Causes springs,
> What mighty Contests rise from trivial Things. (i. 1–2)

This is, of course, the mock-heroic discrepancy. But we miss much of the joke unless we see how near true epic it is. The first line, while nicely suited to Pope's poem, would also fit the passions roused by the rape of Helen, or Agamemnon's seizure of Briseis from Achilles at the opening of *The Iliad*. Then the phrase "am'rous Causes," in the first line, modulates into "trivial Things" in the second. A slight change, masked by rhythm and syntax: but it marks the shift from a possibly epic tension to the full mock-epic discrepancy. The meeting of heroic and trivial in the poem is as often a matter of such subtle transitions as of head-on collision. And there *is* a sense in which even the "mighty Contests . . . trivial Things" discrepancy would fit classical epic: as Pope puts it, in the playfully irreverent "Dedication" to *The Rape*—"the ancient Poets are in one respect like many modern Ladies; Let an Action be never so trivial in it self, they always make it appear of the utmost Importance." The tone of this remark fits parts of the poem like a glove.[3]

But to say that *The Rape of the Lock* contrasts the mighty and the trivial, to the ironic disparagement of the latter, is not enough, even if we recognise how slight the shift from epic grandeur to mock-epic absurdity may be. We must not reduce to one set of terms a poem largely distinguished, among mock-epics, by the variety of ironic contrasts on which it draws. Along with "mighty-trivial" we need other pairs of contraries—for instance, "heroic-effete," "primitive-sophisticated," "antique-contemporary," "masculine-feminine," "principled-opportunistic," "dramatic-histrionic." And although these contrasts work largely in favour of "the ancient Poets" and at the expense of "modern Ladies," this is not always the case. The gap between the contraries is very variable, from the broadest burlesque of heroic ire in Sir Plume's bluster—

> Plague on't! 'tis past a Jest—nay prithee, Pox! (iv. 129)—

to Clarissa's rational appeal for sense and good humour, which in part withstands comparison with its "source," Sarpedon's ringing cry to

---

[3] Epic poets themselves are intermittently aware of the discrepancy. Cf. the description of Satan in Chaos, *Paradise Lost*, ii. 920 ff.:

> Nor was his eare less peal'd
> With noises loud and ruinous (to compare
> Great things with small) than when *Bellona* storms . . .

battle in *The Iliad* (Book XII). There are many times when one feels
not so much that Belinda's world is disparagingly contrasted with a
more "considerable," incomparably wider one, as that the world of
Homer and Virgil has been scaled down, wittily and affectionately, to
admit the *boudoir* and the coffee-table. In other words, the gap between the two worlds can in this poem be ironically exploited to
favour either side, or even both sides at once; it can remain more or
less neutral, simply funny; and it can be closed, whether ludicrously,
in that the Poets and the Ladies share a taste for ostentation, or seriously, in that Agamemnon—

> Till Time shall rifle ev'ry youthful Grace,
> And Age dismiss her from my cold Embrace   (*Iliad,* i. 41–2)—

and Clarissa—

> But since, alas! frail Beauty must decay,
> Curl'd or uncurl'd, since Locks will turn to grey   (v. 25–6)—

bow to a common denominator.

To some of the qualities of Belinda's world, and some of the values
it respects, the poem itself bears witness, taking on the urbanity, polish
and "graceful Ease" which her society accomplished at its best. It is,
to adopt a line of Pope's, "Form'd to delight at once and lash the age"
(*Epitaph on John Gay*). In the finesse of Pope's couplets is mirrored a
cultivated dexterity and poise; his good-natured wit is a virtue of sophisticated, urbane conversation. It is true, of course, that these qualities are in part simply the mask for the poem's assault on a society preoccupied with the superficial, just as that society itself tended to
disguise ugly realities under a prepossessing exterior. One of its earliest
critics commented, shrewdly, "Pope here appears in the light of a man
of gallantry, and of a thorough knowledge of the world." [4] If the poem
assaults the *beau monde,* the attack is mostly good-humoured and
tempered by a sense of the attractiveness of those whose failings are
satirised, a sense of what delicacy, ceremony and elegance could mean
at best.

Its delicacy is the most engaging feature of Belinda's world. What
she prizes glitters as only the ephemeral and the exquisite can. Her
moment of gracefulness, beauty and universal conquest is penultimate.
The poise her society so prizes is nourished by tension—and here
again the poem mirrors as well as criticises, in the perpetual interplay
of poise and tension in Pope's couplets. In the recognition of this
fragility, the necessary frailty and transience of the beautiful, the gap

[4] Joseph Warton, *Essay on the Writings and Genius of Pope,* 1756, p. 246.

between heroic and nonheroic is closed. The epic omens fore-shadowing the loss of Belinda's curls are not entirely hollow, the epic laments over human impermanence are poignant in this context as in Homer. Pope is not merely setting the loss of a mere lock of hair in ironic perspective through the mock-heroic mechanism: he is, para-doxically, touching it with seriousness. In this poem the transience of the ephemeral is moving. The "mighty Contests" are not mighty; but the loss of the lock is not simply a "trivial Thing."

This all amounts to noticing once again, as a reader of the poem can hardly fail to notice, that it runs, with a self-delighting dexterity, through a wide range of attitudes, commanding a startling variety of tones. These features should emerge in analysis. In the meantime, it is important to recognise the essential complexity—in some cases, the ambivalence—of Pope's attitudes to the contrasted worlds of Homer and Belinda. His attitudes to classical epic are partly conditioned by, partly independent of, his reading of Homer's commentators and critics. His attitudes to the *beau monde* are formed partly from ob-servation, partly from the critiques already offered by the Restora-tion dramatists and the periodical essayists. Both worlds had, for Pope and his audience, special defining characteristics. As a translator of Homer, Pope turned to his purpose the special "heroick" idiom which he found best exemplified in Dryden's *Aeneid*. As a critic of Homer, he used the special set of terms accepted for the discussion of epic—as the "Dedication" slyly puts it, "The *Machinery*, Madam, is a Term invented by the Criticks." As a portrayer of upper-class man-ners, he used the anatomised figures (prude, rake and coquette) and the modish language (*"Wounds, Charms,* and *Ardors"*) already fa-miliar to readers and theatre-goers as contemporary "types" and cur-rent absurdities.

These are only a few elements in, so to speak, the "significant soil" which nourishes that vigorous and, in the end, independent plant, the poem. *The Rape of the Lock,* though deeply rooted in its own time, can be read and enjoyed with comparatively little explanatory annota-tion; but full understanding can be built up only from a sense of the unique moment in which it occurs. It is a moment of great interest in the course of neo-classicism, and in the history of the epic itself. Here is a mock-epic written by a poet who had an ambition to write an epic of his own, and whose translation of *The Iliad* has recently been called "the last nonsatiric poem of the European heroic tradi-tion." [5] It is a complex, precarious moment, a point of intersection for a whole web of attitudes and sympathies.

[5] [Douglas] Knight [*Pope and the Heroic Tradition: A Critical Study of His Iliad* (New Haven, 1951)], p. 107.

This is, then, a perpetually surprising poem, a trap for those who label it or who treat it consistently seriously or with consistent levity. It asks of its reader a continuous alert responsiveness: a readiness to laugh on one page at Sir Fopling's operatic *cliché "Those Eyes are made so killing"* (v. 64), while catching the element of serious homage in Pope's reference to "all the Murders" of Belinda's eyes (v. 145); a willingness to be startled by the sudden irruption into the prevailing tone of exuberant, urbane mockery, of something far more astringent—

> The hungry Judges soon the Sentence sign,
> And Wretches hang that Jury-men may dine. (iii. 21–2)

An irrepressible *jeu d'esprit,* the poem is also a serious anatomy of "polite" behaviour, and probes the ageless hurts and pretences of the sex war. A mimicry of epic that would have delighted Martin Scriblerus, it draws on an intimate knowledge of, and full sympathy with, the Renaissance epic ideal. Above all, this is the mock-epic of a mock-world, the make-believe celebration of a society of play-actors. In Belinda's charmed microcosm, where the privileged carry on the masquerade of social ritual and intrigue, there are no worse penalties than prolonged spinsterhood or loss of "face." What *they* think—"the horrid things they say" (iv. 108)—sways action much more easily than a sense of principle or honour. Honour itself has dwindled to mean mere reputation.

And yet Pope makes the predicament Belinda finds herself in, and the penalties she dreads, vividly present to our imaginative sympathy. Observing with dispassion, we are also compelled to respond with feeling intelligence. Some of the poem's hyperboles are neither humorous nor satiric, but sincere. And if an ironic innuendo undercuts a compliment, there is nevertheless a level on which the compliment engagingly survives:

> If to her share some Female Errors fall,
> Look on her Face, and you'll forget 'em all. (ii. 17–18)

This couplet is also a nice example of Pope's adroitness as a reviser of his own work: its fine balance was achieved only when he substituted the milder word "forget" for the outright "forgive" of the early version. Forgiveness was too much to promise, even in jest.

The Case of Miss Arabella Fermor

by Cleanth Brooks

Aldous Huxley's lovers, "quietly sweating, palm to palm," may be conveniently taken to mark the nadir of Petrarchianism. The mistress is no longer a goddess—not even by courtesy. She is a congeries of biological processes and her too evident mortality is proclaimed at every pore. But if we seem to reach, with Huxley's lines, the end of something, it is well to see what it is that has come to an end. It is not the end of a naïve illusion.

The Elizabethans, even those who were immersed in the best tradition of Petrarchianism, did not have to wait upon the advent of modern science to find out that women perspired. They were thoroughly aware that woman was a biological organism, but their recognition of this fact did not prevent them from asserting, on occasion, that she was a goddess, nevertheless. John Donne, for instance, frequently has it both ways: indeed, some of the difficulty which the modern reader has with his poems may reside in the fact that he sometimes has it both ways in the same poem. What is relevant to our purposes here is not the occurrence of a line like "Such are the sweat drops of my Mistres breast" in one of the satiric "elegies," but the occurrence of lines like

> Our hands were firmly cimented
> With a fast balme, which thence did spring

in a poem like "The Ecstasy"! The passage quoted, one may argue, glances at the very phenomenon which Huxley so amiably describes; but Donne has transmuted it into something else.

But if Donne could have it both ways, most of us, in this latter day, cannot. We are disciplined in the tradition of either-or, and lack the mental agility—to say nothing of the maturity of attitude—which would allow us to indulge in the finer distinctions and the more subtle reservations permitted by the tradition of both-and. Flesh *or* spirit, merely a doxy or purely a goddess (or alternately, one and then the other), is more easily managed in our poetry, and probably, for that matter, in our private lives. But the greater poems of our tradition are more ambitious in this matter: as a consequence, they come perhaps nearer the truth than we do with our ordinary hand-to-mouth insights. In saying this, however, one need by no means confine himself to the poetry of Donne. If we are not too much blinded by our doctrine of either-or, we shall be able to see that there are many poems in the English tradition which demonstrate a thorough awareness of the problem and which manage, at their appropriate levels, the same kinds of synthesis of attitudes which we associate characteristically with Donne.

Take Pope's *Rape of the Lock*, for instance. Is Belinda a goddess, or is she merely a frivolous tease? Pope himself was, we may be sure, thoroughly aware of the problem. His friend Swift penetrated the secrets of the lady's dressing room with what results we know. Belinda's dressing table, of course, is bathed in a very different atmosphere; yet it may be significant that Pope is willing to allow us to observe his heroine at her dressing table at all. The poet definitely means to give us scenes from the greenroom, and views from the wings, as well as a presentation "in character" on the lighted stage.

Pope, of course, did not write *The Rape of the Lock* because he was obsessed with the problem of Belinda's divinity. He shows, indeed, that he was interested in a great many things: in various kinds of social satire, in a playful treatment of the epic manner, in deflating some of the more vapid clichés that filled the love poetry of the period, and in a dozen other things. But we are familiar with Pope's interest in the mock-epic as we are not familiar with his interest in the problem of woman as goddess; and moreover, the rather lurid conventional picture of Pope as the "wicked wasp of Twickenham"—the particular variant of the either-or theory as applied to Pope—encourages us to take the poem as a dainty but rather obvious satire. There is some justification, therefore, for emphasizing aspects of the poem which have received little attention in the past, and perhaps for neglecting other aspects of the poem which critics have already treated in luminous detail.

One further point should be made: if Pope in this account of the poem turns out to be something of a symbolist poet, and perhaps even something of what we call, in our clumsy phrase, a "metaphysical poet" as well, we need not be alarmed. It matters very little whether or not we twist some of the categories which the literary historian jealously (and perhaps properly) guards. It matters a great deal that we understand Pope's poem in its full richness and complexity. It would be an amusing irony (and one not wholly undeserved) if we retorted upon Pope some of the brittleness and inelasticity which we feel that Pope was inclined to impose upon the more fluid and illogical poetry which preceded him. But the real victims of the maneuver, if it blinded us to his poem, would be ourselves.

Pope's own friends were sometimes guilty of oversimplifying and reducing his poem by trying to make it accord with a narrow and pedantic logic. For example, Bishop Warburton, Pope's friend and editor, finds an error in the famous passage in which Belinda and her maid are represented as priestesses invoking the goddess of beauty. Warburton feels forced to comment as follows: "There is a small inaccuracy in these lines. He first makes his Heroine the chief Priestess, then the Goddess herself." The lines in question run as follows:

> First, rob'd in White, the Nymph intent adores
> With Head uncover'd, the *Cosmetic* Pow'rs.
> A heav'nly Image in the Glass appears,
> To that she bends, to that her Eyes she rears . . .

It is true that Pope goes on to imply that Belinda is the chief priestess (by calling her maid the "inferior Priestess"), and that, a few lines later, he has the maid deck the goddess (Belinda) "with the glitt'ring Spoil." But surely Warburton ought not to have missed the point: Belinda, in worshiping at the shrine of beauty, quite naturally worships herself. Whose else is the "heav'nly Image" which appears in the mirror to which she raises her eyes? The violation of logic involved is intended and is thoroughly justified. Belinda *is* a goddess, but she puts on her divinity at her dressing table; and, such is the paradox of beauty-worship, she can be both the sincere devotee and the divinity herself. We shall certainly require more sensitive instruments than Bishop Warburton's logic if we are to become aware of some of the nicest effects in the poem.

But to continue with the dressing-table scene:

> The Fair each moment rises in her Charms,
> Repairs her Smiles, awakens ev'ry Grace,
> And calls forth all the Wonders of her Face;
> Sees by Degrees a purer Blush arise,
> And keener Lightnings quicken in her Eyes.

It is the experience which the cosmetic advertisers take at a level of dead seriousness, and obviously Pope is amused to have it taken seriously. And yet, is there not more here than the obvious humor? Belinda is, after all, an artist, and who should be more sympathetic with the problems of the conscious artist than Pope himself? In our own time, William Butler Yeats, a less finicky poet than Pope, could address a "young beauty" as "dear fellow artist."

In particular, consider the "purer Blush." Why purer? One must not laugh too easily at the purity of the blush which Belinda is engaged in painting upon her face. After all, may we not regard it as a blush "recollected in tranquillity," and therefore a more ideal blush than the spontaneous actual blush which shame or hauteur on an actual occasion might bring? If we merely read "purer" as ironic for its opposite, "impurer"—that is, unspontaneous and therefore unmaidenly—we shall miss not only the more delightful aspects of the humor, but we shall miss also Pope's concern for the real problem. Which is, after all, the more maidenly blush? That will depend, obviously, upon what one considers the essential nature of maidens to be; and Belinda, we ought to be reminded, is not the less real nor the less feminine because she fails to resemble Whittier's robust heroine, Maude Muller.

One is tempted to insist upon these ambiguities and complexities of attitude, not with any idea of overturning the orthodox reading of Pope's irony, but rather to make sure that we do not conceive it to be more brittle and thin than it actually is. This fact, at least, should be plain: regardless of what we may make of the "purer Blush," it is true that Belinda's dressing table does glow with a special radiance and charm, and that Pope, though amused by the vanity which it represents, is at the same time thoroughly alive to a beauty which it actually possesses.

There is a further reason for feeling that we shall not err in taking the niceties of Pope's descriptions quite seriously. One notices that even the metaphors by which Pope characterizes Belinda are not casual bits of decoration, used for a moment, and then forgotten. They run throughout the poem as if they were motifs. For instance, at her dressing table Belinda is not only a priestess of "the Sacred Rites of Pride," but she is also compared to a warrior arming for the fray. Later in the poem she is the warrior once more at the card table in her conquest of the two "adventrous Knights"; and again, at the end of the poem, she emerges as the heroic conqueror in the epic encounter of the beaux and belles.

To take another example, Belinda, early in the poem, is compared to the sun. Pope suggests that the sun recognizes in Belinda a rival, and fears her:

> *Sol* thro' white Curtains shot a tim'rous Ray,
> And op'd those Eyes that must eclipse the Day.

But the sun's fear of Belinda has not been introduced merely in order to give the poet an opportunity to mock at the polite cliché. The sun comparison appears again at the beginning of Canto II:

> Not with more Glories, in th' Etherial Plain,
> The Sun first rises o'er the purpled Main,
> Than issuing forth, the Rival of his Beams
> Lanch'd on the Bosom of the silver *Thames.*

Belinda is like the sun, not only because of her bright eyes, and not only because she dominates her special world ("But ev'ry Eye was fix'd on her alone"). She is like the sun in another regard:

> Bright as the Sun, her Eyes the Gazers strike,
> And, like the Sun, they shine on all alike.

Is this general munificence on the part of Belinda a fault or a virtue? Is she shallow and flirtatious, giving her favors freely to all; or, does she distribute her largesse impartially like a great prince? Or, is she simply the well-bred belle who knows that she cannot play favorites if she wishes to be popular? The sun comparison is able to carry all these meanings, and therefore goes past any momentary jest. Granting that it may be overingenious to argue that Belinda in Canto IV (the gloomy Cave of Spleen) represents the sun in eclipse, still the sun comparison does appear once more in the poem, and quite explicitly. As the poem closes, Pope addresses Belinda thus:

> When those fair Suns shall sett, as sett they must,
> And all those Tresses shall be laid in Dust;
> *This Lock,* the Muse shall consecrate to Fame,
> And mid'st the stars inscribe *Belinda's* Name!

Here, one notices that the poet, if he is forced to concede that Belinda's eyes are only metaphorical suns after all, still promises that the ravished lock shall have a celestial eternity, adding, like the planet Venus, "new Glory to the shining Sphere!" And here Pope, we may be sure, is not merely playful in his metaphor. Belinda's name has been inscribed in the only heaven in which a poet would care to inscribe it. If the skeptic still has any doubts about Pope's taking Belinda very seriously, there should be no difficulty in convincing him that Pope took his own work very seriously indeed.

We began by raising the question of Belinda's status as a goddess.

It ought to be quite clear that Pope's attitude toward Belinda is not exhausted in laughing away her claims to divinity. The attitude is much more complicated than that. Belinda's charm is not viewed uncritically, but the charm is real: it can survive the poet's knowledge of how much art and artifice have gone into making up the charm. The attitude is not wholly unrelated to that of Mirabell toward Millamant in Congreve's *The Way of the World*. Mirabell knows that his mistress has her faults, but as he philosophically remarks: ". . . I like her with all her faults; nay, like her for her faults. Her follies are so natural, or so artful, that they become her. . . . she once used me with that insolence, that in revenge I took her to pieces, sifted her, and separated her failings; I studied 'em, and got 'em by rote. . . . They are now grown as familiar to me as my own frailties; and in all probability, in a little time longer, I shall like 'em as well." The relation of author to creation can be more philosophical still: and though Pope's attitude toward his heroine has a large element of amused patronage in it, I find no contempt. Rather, Pope finds Belinda charming, and expects us to feel her charm.

To pursue the matter of attitude further still, what, after all, is Pope's attitude toward the iridescent little myth of the sylphs which he has provided to symbolize the polite conventions which govern the conduct of maidens? We miss the whole point if we dismiss the sylphs as merely "supernatural machinery." In general, we may say that the myth represents a qualification of the poet's prevailingly naturalistic interpretation. More specifically, it represents his attempt to do justice to the intricacies of the feminine mind. For, in spite of Pope's amusement at the irrationality of that mind, Pope acknowledges its beauty and its power.

In making this acknowledgement, he is a good realist—a better realist, indeed, than he appears when he tries to parade the fashionable ideas of the Age of Reason as in his "Essay on Man." He is good enough realist to know that although men in their "Learned Pride" may say that it is Honor which protects the chastity of maids, actually it is nothing of the sort: the belles are not kept chaste by any mere abstraction. It is the sylphs, the sylphs with their interest in fashion notes and their knowledge of the feminine heart:

> With varying Vanities, from ev'ry Part,
> They shift the moving Toyshop of their Heart;
> Where Wigs with Wigs, with Sword-knots Sword-
>   knots strive,
> Beaus banish beaus, and Coaches Coaches drive.

Yet the myth of the sylphs is no mere decoration to this essentially cynical generalization. The sylphs do represent the supernatural, though the supernatural reduced, of course, to its flimsiest proportions. The poet has been very careful here. Even Belinda is not made to take their existence too seriously. As for the poet, he very modestly excuses himself from rendering any judgment at all by ranging himself on the side of "Learned Pride":

> Some secret Truths from Learned Pride conceal'd,
> To Maids alone and Children are reveal'd:
> What tho' no Credit doubting Wits may give?
> The Fair and Innocent shall still believe.

In the old wives' tale or the child's fairy story may lurk an item of truth, after all. Consider the passage carefully.

"Fair" and "Innocent" balance "Maids" and "Children." Yet they act further to color the whole passage. Is "fair" used merely as a synonym for "maids"—e.g., as in "the fair"? Or, is it that beauty is easily flattered? The doctrine which Ariel urges Belinda to accept is certainly flattering: "Hear and believe! thy own Importance know/ . . . unnumber'd Spirits round thee fly. . . ." Is "innocent" to be taken to mean "guiltless," or does it mean "naïve," perhaps even "credulous"? And how do "fair" and "innocent" influence each other? Do the fair believe in the sylphs because they are still children? (Ariel, one remembers, begins by saying: "If e'er one Vision touch'd thy *infant* Thought . . .") Pope is here exploiting that whole complex of associations which surround "innocence" and connect it on the one hand with more than worldly wisdom and, on the other, with simple gullibility.

Pope, as we now know, was clearly unjust in suggesting that Addison's advice against adding the machinery of the sylphs was prompted by any desire to prevent the improvement of the poem. Addison's caution was "safe" and natural under the circumstances. But we can better understand Pope's pique if we come to understand how important the machinery was to become in the final version of the poem. For it is Pope's treatment of the sylphs which allows him to develop, with the most delicate modulation, his whole attitude toward Belinda and the special world which she graces. It is precisely the poet's handling of the supernatural—the level at which he is willing to entertain it— the amused qualifications which he demands of it—that makes it possible for him to state his attitude with full complexity.

The sylphs are, as Ariel himself suggests, "honor," though honor rendered concrete and as it actually functions, not honor as a dry abstraction. The sylphs' concern for good taste allows little range for critical perspective or a sense of proportion. To Ariel it will really be a dire disaster whether it is her honor or her new brocade that Belinda stains. To stain her honor will certainly constitute a breach of good taste—whatever else it may be—and that for Ariel is enough. Indeed, it is enough for the rather artificial world of manners with which Pope is concerned.

The myth of the sylphs is, thus, of the utmost utility to Pope: it allows him to show his awareness of the absurdities of a point of view which, nevertheless, is charming, delightful, and filled with a real poetry. Most important of all, the myth allows him to suggest that the charm, in part at least, springs from the very absurdity. The two elements can hardly be separated in Belinda; in her guardian, Ariel, they cannot be separated at all.

In this connection, it is well to raise specifically the question of Pope's attitude toward the "rape" itself. We certainly underestimate the poem if we rest complacently in the view that Pope is merely laughing at a tempest in a teapot. There is such laughter, to be sure, and late in the poem, Pope expresses his own judgment of the situation, employing Clarissa as his mouthpiece. But the tempest, ridiculous though it is when seen in perspective, is a real enough tempest and related to very real issues. Indeed, Pope is able to reduce the incident to its true importance, precisely because he recognizes clearly its hidden significance. And nowhere is Pope more careful to take into account all the many sides of the situation than just here in the loss of the lock itself.

For one thing, Pope is entirely too clear-sighted to allow that the charming Belinda is merely the innocent victim of a rude assault. Why has she cherished the lock at all? In part at least, "to the Destruction of Mankind," though mankind, of course, in keeping with the convention, wishes so to be destroyed. Pope suggests that the Baron may even be the victim rather than the aggressor—it is a moot question whether he has seized the lock or been ensnared by it. Pope does this very skillfully, but with great emphasis:

> Love in these Labyrinths his Slaves detains,
> And mighty Hearts are held in slender Chains.
> With hairy Sprindges we the Birds betray,
> Slight Lines of Hair surprize the Finny Prey,
> Fair Tresses Man's Imperial Race insnare,
> And Beauty draws us with a single Hair.

Indeed, at the end of the poem, the poet addresses his heroine not as victim but as a "murderer":

> For, after all the Murders of your Eye,
> When, after Millions slain, your self shall die. . . .

After all, does not Belinda want the Baron (and young men in general) to covet the lock? She certainly does not want to retain possession of the lock forever. The poet naturally sympathizes with Belinda's pique at the way in which the Baron obtains the lock. He must, in the war of the sexes, coax her into letting him have it. Force is clearly unfair, though blandishment is fair. If she is an able warrior, she will consent to the young man's taking the lock, though the lock still attached to her head—and on the proper terms, honorable marriage. If she is a weak opponent, she will yield the lock, and herself, without any stipulation of terms, and will thus become a ruined maid indeed. Pope has absolutely no illusions about what the game is, and is certainly not to be shocked by any naturalistic interpretation of the elaborate and courtly conventions under which Belinda fulfills her natural function of finding a mate.

On the other hand, this is not at all to say that Pope is anxious to do away with the courtly conventions as a pious fraud. He is not the romantic anarchist who would abolish all conventions because they are artificial. The conventions not only have a regularizing function: they have their own charm. Like the rules of the card game in which Belinda triumphs, they may at points be arbitrary; but they make the game possible, and with it, the poetry and pageantry involved in it, in which Pope very clearly delights.

The card game itself, of course, is another symbol of the war of the sexes. Belinda must defeat the men; she must avoid that debacle in which

> The *Knave* of *Diamonds* tries his wily Arts,
> And wins (oh shameful Chance!) the *Queen* of *Hearts.*

She must certainly avoid at every cost becoming a ruined maid. In the game as played, there is a moment in which she is "Just in the Jaws of Ruin, and *Codille*," and gets a thrill of delicious excitement at being in so precarious a position.

If the reader objects that the last comment suggests a too obviously sexual interpretation of the card game, one must hasten to point out that a pervasive sexual symbolism informs, not only the description of the card game, but almost everything else in the poem, though here, again, our tradition of either-or may cause us to miss what Pope is doing. We are not forced to take the poem as either sly bawdy *or* as delightful fantasy. But if we are to see what Pope actually makes of his problem, we shall have to be alive to the sexual implications which are in the poem.

They are perfectly evident—even in the title itself; and the poem begins with an address to the Muse in which the sexual implications are underscored:

> Say what strange Motive, Goddess! cou'd compel
> A well-bred Lord t'assault a gentle *Belle?*
> Oh say what stranger Cause, yet unexplor'd,
> Cou'd make a gentle *Belle* reject a *Lord?*

True, we can take *assault* and *reject* in their more general meanings, not in their specific Latin senses, but the specific meanings are there just beneath the surface. Indeed, it is hard to believe, on the evidence of the poem as a whole, that Pope would have been in the least surprised by Sir James Frazer's later commentaries on the ubiquity of hair as a fertility symbol. In the same way, one finds it hard to believe, after some of the material in the "Cave of Spleen" section ("And Maids turn'd Bottels, call aloud for Corks"), that Pope would have been too much startled by the theories of Sigmund Freud.

The sexual implications become quite specific after the "rape" has occurred. Thalestris, in inciting Belinda to take action against the Baron, cries:

> Gods! shall the Ravisher display your Hair,
> While the Fops envy, and the Ladies stare!

Even if we take *ravisher* in its most general sense, still the sexual symbolism lurks just behind Thalestris' words. Else why should honor be involved as it is? Why should the Baron desire the lock, and why should Belinda object so violently, not as to an act of simple rudeness, but to losing "honor" and becoming a "degraded Toast"? The sexual element is involved at least to the extent that Belinda feels that she cannot afford to suffer the Baron, without protest, to take such a "liberty."

But a deeper sexual importance is symbolized by the whole incident. Belinda's anguished exclamation—

> Oh hadst thou, Cruel! been content to seize
> Hairs less in sight, or any Hairs but these!

carries on, unconsciously, the sexual suggestion. The lines indicate, primarily, of course, Belinda's exasperation at the ruining of her coiffure. The principal ironic effect, therefore, is one of bathos: her angry concern for the prominence of the lock deflates a little her protests about honor. (Something of the bathos carries over to the sexual parallel: it is hinted, perhaps, that the worst thing about a real rape for the belle would be that it could not be concealed.) But though Belinda's vehemence gives rise to these ironies, the exclamation itself is dramatically appropriate; and Belinda would doubtless have blushed to have her emphasis on "any" interpreted literally and rudely. In her anger, she is obviously unconscious of the *faux pas*. But the fops whose admiring and envious comments on the exposed trophy Thalestris can predict—"Already hear the horrid things they say"—would be thoroughly alive to the unconscious *double entendre*. Pope's friend, Matthew Prior, wrote a naughty poem in which the same *double entendre* occurs. Pope himself, we may be sure, was perfectly aware of it.

In commenting on Pope's attitude toward the rape, we have suggested by implication his attitude toward chastity. Chastity is one of Belinda's most becoming garments. It gives her her retinue of airy guardians. As a proper maiden, she will keep from staining it just as she will keep from staining her new brocade. Its very fragility is part of its charm, and Pope becomes something of a symbolist poet in suggesting this. Three times in the poem he refers to the breaking of a frail china jar, once in connection with the loss of chastity, twice in connection with the loss of "honor" suffered by Belinda in the "rape" of the lock:

> Whether the Nymph shall break *Diana's* Law,
> Or some frail *China* Jar receive a Flaw. . . .

> Or when rich *China* Vessels, fal'n from high,
> In glitt'ring Dust and painted Fragments lie!

> Thrice from my trembling hands the *Patch-box* fell;
> The tott'ring *China* shook without a Wind. . . .

Pope does not say, but he suggests, that chastity is, like the fine porcelain, something brittle, precious, useless, and easily broken. In the same way, he has hinted that honor (for which the sylphs, in part, stand) is something pretty, airy, fluid, and not really believed in. The devoted sylph who interposes his "body" between the lock and the closing shears is clipped in two, but honor suffers little damage:

> Fate urg'd the Sheers, and cut the *Sylph* in twain,
> (But Airy Substance soon unites again).

It would be easy here to turn Pope into a cynic; but to try to do this is to miss the point. Pope does not hold chastity to be of no account. He definitely expects Belinda to be chaste; but, as a good humanist, he evidently regards virginity as essentially a negative virtue, and its possession, a temporary state. He is very far from associating it with any magic virtue as Milton does in his *Comus.* The only magic which he will allow it is a kind of charm—a *je-ne-sais-quoi* such as the sylphs possess.

Actually, we probably distort Pope's views by putting the question in terms which require an explicit judgment at all. Pope accepts in the poem the necessity for the belle to be chaste just as he accepts the necessity for her to be gracious and attractive. But in accepting this, he is thoroughly alive to the cant frequently talked about woman's honor, and most of all, he is ironically, though quietly, resolute in putting first things first. This, I take it, is the whole point of Clarissa's speech. When Clarissa says:

> Since painted, or not painted, all shall fade,
> And she who scorns a Man, must die a Maid,

we need not assume with Leslie Stephen that Pope is expressing a smug masculine superiority, with the implication that, for a woman, spinsterhood is the worst of all possible ills. (There is actually no reason for supposing that Pope thought it so.) The real point is that, for Belinda, perpetual spinsterhood *is* the worst of all possible ills. In her own terms, it would be a disaster to retain her locks forever—locks turned to gray, though still curled with a pathetic hopefulness, unclaimed and unpossessed by any man. Belinda does not want *that;* and it is thus a violation of good sense to lose sight of the fact that the cherished lock is finally only a means to an end—one weapon to be used by the warrior in the battle, and not the strongest weapon at that.

Clarissa is, of course, promptly called a prude, and the battle begins at once in perfect disregard of the "good sense" that she has spoken. Pope is too fine an artist to have it happen otherwise. Belinda *has* been sorely vexed—and she, moreover, remains charming, even as an Amazon. After all, what the poet has said earlier is sincerely meant:

> If to her share some Female Errors fall,
> Look on her Face, and you'll forget 'em all.

Though Pope obviously agrees with Clarissa, he is neither surprised nor particularly displeased with his heroine for flying in the face of Clarissa's advice.

The battle of the sexes which ensues parodies at some points the combat in the great epic which Milton fashioned on the rape of the apple. But the absurdity of a battle in which the contestants cannot be killed is a flaw in Milton's great poem, whereas Pope turns it to beautiful account in his. In *Paradise Lost,* the great archangels single each other out for combat in the best Homeric style. But when Michael's sword cleaves the side of Lucifer, the most that Milton can do with the incident is to observe that Lucifer feels pain, for his premises force him to hurry on to admit that

> . . . th'Ethereal substance clos'd
> Not long divisible. . . .

Lucifer is soon back in the fight, completely hale and formidable as ever. We have already seen how delightfully Pope converts this cabbage into a rose in the incident in which the sylph, in a desperate defense of the lock, is clipped in two by the shears.

The absurdity of a war fought by invulnerable opponents gives an air of unreality to the whole of Milton's episode. There is a bickering over rules. Satan and his followers cheat by inventing gunpowder. The hosts under Michael retort by throwing the celestial hills at the enemy; and the Almighty, to put a stop to the shameful rumpus, has the Son throw the troublemakers out. But if the fight were really serious, a fight to the death, why does the heavenly host not throw the hills in the first place? Or, why does not the Almighty cast out the rebels without waiting for the three days of inconclusive fighting to elapse? The prevailing atmosphere of a game—a game played by good little boys and by unmannerly little ruffians, a game presided over by the stern schoolmaster—haunts the whole episode. The advantage is wholly with Pope here. By frankly recognizing that the contest between his beaux and belles is a game, he makes for his basic intention.

The suspicion that Pope in this episode is glancing at Milton is corroborated somewhat by Pope's general use of his celestial machinery. The supernatural guardians in *The Rape of the Lock* are made much of, but their effectiveness is hardly commensurate with their zeal. The affinities of the poem on this point are again with *Paradise Lost,* not with the *Iliad.* In Milton's poem, the angels are carefully stationed to guard Adam and Eve in their earthly home, but their protection proves, in the event, to be singularly ineffectual. They cannot prevent Satan from finding his way to the earth; and though they soar over the Garden, their "radiant Files,/Daz'ling the Moon," they never strike a blow. Even when they discover Satan, and prepare to engage him in combat, God, at the last moment, prevents the fight. Indeed, for all their numbers and for all their dazzling splendor, they succeed in determining events not at all. They can merely, in the case of Raphael, give the human pair advice and warning. Milton, though he loved to call their resonant names, and evidently tried to provide them with a realistic function, was apparently so fearful lest he divert attention from Adam's own freely made decision that he succeeds in giving them nothing to do.

If this limitation constitutes another ironical defect, perhaps, in Milton's great epic, it fits Pope's purposes beautifully. For, as we have seen, Pope's supernatural machinery is as airy as gossamer, and the fact that Ariel can do no more than Raphael, advise and warn—for all his display of zeal—makes again for Pope's basic intention. The issues in Pope's poem are matters of taste, matters of "good sense," and the sylphs do not violate the human limitations of this world which Pope has elected to describe and in terms of which judgments are to be made. Matters of morality—still less, the ultimate sanctions of morality—are never raised.

One more of the numerous parallels between *The Rape of the Lock* and *Paradise Lost* ought to be mentioned here, even though it may well be one of which Pope was unconscious. After the Fall has taken place, Michael is sent to prepare Adam for his expulsion from the happy garden. The damage has been done, the apple has been plucked and eaten, the human pair must prepare to go out into the "real" world, the "fallen" world of our ordinary human experience. Yet, Michael promises that Adam can create within his own breast "A Paradise . . . happier farr." Clarissa's advice to Belinda makes the same point. For better or worse, the lock has been lost. That fact must be accepted. In suggesting Belinda's best course under the circumstances, Clarissa raises quite explicitly Belinda's status as a divinity:

> Say, why are Beauties prais'd and honour'd most . . .
> Why Angels call'd, and Angel-like ador'd?

The divine element cannot reside in mere beauty alone, painted cheeks, bright eyes, curled locks. All human beauty is tainted with mortality: true "angelhood" resides in a quality of mind, and therefore can survive the loss of mere mortal beauty—can survive the loss of the lock, even the destruction of its beauty by the shears of time. The general parallel between the two speeches is almost complete. Belinda's true divinity, like Adam's happier paradise, is to be found within her. Pope, like Milton, can thus rationalize the matter in terms which allow him to dismiss the supernatural machinery and yet maintain the presence of a qualified supernatural in the midst of a stern and rational world in which no longer one may expect "God or Angel Guest/ With Man, as with his Friend, familiar us'd/ To sit indulgent"—an altered world in which Belinda will expect no more intimate communications from Ariel, and where she, like Adam and Eve, must rely on an inner virtue for advice and protection.

Indeed, one is tempted to complete the parallel by suggesting that Belinda is, at this point, like Adam, being prepared to leave her happy garden world of innocence and maidenly delight for a harsher world, the world of human society as it is and with the poetic illusions removed.

To return to the battle between the beaux and belles: here Pope beautifully unifies the various motifs of the poem. The real nature of the conventions of polite society, the heroic pretensions of that society as mirrored in the epic, the flattering clichés which society conventionally employs—all come in for a genial ragging. Indeed, the clichés of the ardent lover become the focal point of concentration. For the clichés, if they make the contention absurd and pompous, do indicate, by coming alive on another level, the true, if unconscious, nature of the struggle.

> No common Weapons in their Hands are found,
> Like Gods they fight, nor dread a mortal Wound.

"Like Gods they fight" should mean, in the epic framework, "with superhuman energy and valor." And "nor dread a mortal Wound" logically completes "Like Gods they fight"—until a yet sterner logic asserts itself and deflates the epic pomp. A fight in which the opponents cannot be killed is only a sham fight. Yet, this second meaning is very rich after all, and draws "Like Gods they fight" into its own orbit of meanings: there may be an extra zest in the fighting because it *is* an elaborate game. One can make godlike gestures because one has the invulnerability of a god. The contest is godlike, after all, because it is raised above the dust and turmoil of real issues. Like an elaborate dance, it symbolizes real issues but can find room for a grace and poetry which in a more earnest struggle are lost.

I have said earlier that Pope, by recognizing the real issues involved, is able to render his mock-epic battle meaningful. For the beaux of Hampton Court, though in truth they do not need to dread a mortal wound, can, and are prepared to, die. We must remember that "to die" had at this period, as one of its submeanings, to experience the consummation of the sexual act. Pope's invulnerable beaux rush bravely forward to achieve such a death; for the war of the sexes, when fought seriously and to the death, ends in such an act.

The elegant battleground resounds with the cries of those who die "in *Metaphor,* and . . . in *Song.*" In some cases, little more is implied

than a teasing of the popular clichés about bearing a "living Death,"
or being burnt alive in Cupid's flames. But few will question the
sexual implications of "die" in the passage in which Belinda over-
comes the Baron:

> Nor fear'd the Chief th'unequal Fight to try,
> Who sought no more than on his Foe to die. . . .
> "Boast not my Fall" (he cry'd) "insulting Foe!
> Thou by some other shalt be laid as low. . . ."

The point is not that Pope is here leering at bawdy meanings. In
the full context of the poem, they are not bawdy at all—or, perhaps
we put the matter more accurately if we say that Pope's *total* attitude,
as reflected in the poem, is able to absorb and digest into itself the
incidental bawdy of which Pope's friends, and obviously Pope himself,
were conscious. The crucial point is that Pope's interpretation of
Belinda's divinity does not need to flinch from bawdy interpretations.
The further meanings suggested by the naughty *double entendres*
are not merely snickering jibes which contradict the surface meaning:
rather those further meanings constitute the qualifying background
against which Belinda's divinity is asserted. Pope's testimony to Belinda's charm is not glib; it is not thin and one-sided. It is qualified
by, though not destroyed by, a recognition of all the factors involved
—even of those factors which seem superficially to negate it. The
touch is light, to be sure; but the poem is not flimsy, not mere froth.
The tone is ironical, but the irony is not that of a narrow and acerb
satire; rather it is an irony which accords with a wise recognition of
the total situation. The "form" of the poem is, therefore, much more
than the precise regard for a set of rules and conventions mechanically
apprehended. It is, finally, the delicate balance and reconciliation of
a host of partial interpretations and attitudes.

It was observed earlier that Pope is able to reduce the "rape" to its
true insignificance because he recognizes, as his characters do not, its
real significance. Pope knows that the rape has in it more of compliment than of insult, though he naturally hardly expects Belinda to
interpret it thus. He does not question her indignation, but he does
suggest that it is, perhaps, a more complex response than Belinda
realizes. Pope knows too how artificial the social conventions really are
and he is thoroughly cognizant of the economic and biological neces-
sities which underlie them—which the conventions sometimes seem
to mask and sometimes to adorn. He is therefore not forced to choose
between regarding them as either a hypocritical disguise or as a poetic
and graceful adornment. Knowing their true nature, he can view

this outrage of the conventions with a wise and amused tolerance, and can set it in its proper perspective.

Here the functional aspect of Pope's choice of the epic framework becomes plain. The detachment, the amused patronage, the note of aloof and impartial judgment—all demand that the incident be viewed with a large measure of aesthetic distance. Whatever incidental fun Pope may have had with the epic conventions, his choice of the mock-epic fits beautifully his general problem of scaling down the rape to its proper insignificance. The scene is reduced and the characters become small and manageable figures whose actions can always be plotted against a larger background.

How large that background is has not always been noticed. Belinda's world is plainly a charming, artificial world; but Pope is not afraid to let in a glimpse of the real world which lies all about it:

> Mean while declining from the Noon of Day,
> The Sun obliquely shoots his burning Ray;
> The hungry Judges soon the Sentence sign,
> And Wretches hang that Jury-men may Dine;
> The Merchant from th'*Exchange* returns in Peace,
> And the long Labours of the *Toilette* cease—
> *Belinda* now . . .

It is a world in which business goes on and criminals are hanged for all that Belinda is preparing to sit down to ombre. This momentary glimpse of the world of serious affairs, of the world of business and law, of the world of casualness and cruelty, is not introduced merely to shrivel the high concerns of polite society into ironical insignificance, though its effect, of course, is to mock at the seriousness with which the world of fashion takes its affairs. Nor is the ironical clash which is introduced by the passage uncalculated and unintentional: it is not that Pope himself is unconsciously callous—without sympathy for the "wretches." The truth is that Pope's own perspective is so scaled, his totality of view so honest, that he can afford to embellish his little drama as lovingly as he likes without for a moment losing sight of its final triviality. A lesser poet would either have feared to introduce an echo of the "real" world lest the effect prove to be too discordant, or would have insisted on the discord and moralized, too heavily and bitterly, the contrast between the gay and the serious. Pope's tact is perfect. The passage is an instance of the complexity of tone which the poem possesses.

A Complex Mock-Heroic:
The Rape of the Lock

by Ian Jack

If the Moderns have excelled the Ancients in any species of
writing, it seems to be in satire: and, particularly in that kind
of satire, which is conveyed in the form of the epopee. . . .
As the poet disappears in this way of writing, and does not
deliver the intended censure in his own proper person, the
satire becomes more delicate, because more oblique. Add to
this, that a tale or story more strongly engages and interests
the reader, than a series of precepts or reproofs, or even of
characters themselves, however lively and natural. An heroi-
comic poem may therefore be justly esteemed the most excellent kind of satire.

JOSEPH WARTON[1]

"The first principle of Criticism," Pope wrote in the postscript to his
translation of the *Odyssey*, "is to consider the nature of the piece,
and the intent of its author." In *The Rape of the Lock* neither is in
doubt. The incident on which the poem is founded had caused a
breach between the two families of the Petres and the Fermors, and it
was suggested to Pope that he should help "to make a jest of it, and
laugh them together again."
    The writing of a witty narrative poem was one of the most obvious
methods; and no species of narrative was more eligible than the mock-
heroic, so highly praised by Dryden. It was a genre which had much to
recommend it. It had been evolved for the very purpose of "diminish-

"*A Complex Mock-Heroic:* The Rape of the Lock" *by Ian Jack. From* Augustan
Satire: Intention and Idiom in English Poetry 1660–1750 *(Oxford: Clarendon Press,
1952). Copyright 1952 by the Clarendon Press, Oxford. Reprinted by permission of
the author and publisher. The footnotes of this article have been abridged for the
purposes of this edition.*

[1] *An Essay on the Genius and Writings of Pope. In Two Volumes,* 4th ed. (1782),
I, 211.

ing" petty quarrels, and combined the two sorts of writing in which the age was most interested: epic and satire. And there was still a spice of novelty about it. Rowe had even questioned "if it can be call'd a Kind, that is so new in the World, and of which we have had so few Instances." [2] While *Le Lutrin* and *The Dispensary* (whose composition Pope had followed with keen interest) were suitable models, neither of them was so brilliant as to be discouraging. Pope may well have aspired to write a consummate example of the mock-heroic genre before Lord Petre stole the lock: it may be that in the quarrel of the Petres and the Fermors he merely found matter and opportunity for the attempt.

While modern critics often think of a mock-heroic poem primarily as a satire on the epic,[3] the Augustans laid the emphasis elsewhere. The technical brilliance of *The Rape of the Lock* is largely due to the care with which Pope had studied the great epics and the remarks of the critics with a view to writing an epic of his own. Nor did the success of his mock-epic make a heroic poem seem a less worthy ambition; for he was planning an epic until the last days of his life.

The writers who did ridicule the epic in the Augustan age were the authors of burlesques and travesties; and Dennis was not alone in thinking their object "a very scurvy one." In mock-epic a dignified genre is turned to witty use without being cheapened in any way. The poet has an opportunity of ridiculing through incongruity, and of affording his reader the sophisticated pleasure of recognizing ironical parallels to familiar passages in Homer and Virgil. A mock-heroic poem is a "parody" of the epic, but a parody in the Augustan sense, not in the modern. The "new purpose" of the frequent "allusions" throughout *The Rape of the Lock* is not the ridicule of a literary form but the setting of a lovers' tiff in true perspective.

The fact that the 1712 version of *The Rape of the Lock* consists of no more than 334 lines and takes over only a few of the characteristics of the epic makes it clear that Pope's concern was less with Homer and Virgil than with Miss Fermor and Lord Petre. The style is heroic; but the invocation, the proposition of the subject, the descriptions, the moralizing asides, the speeches and the battle are practically the only structural features modelled on the epic. Clearly the poet's purpose at this stage was neither to ridicule the heroic genre nor to provide a humorous parallel to all the principal ingredients of epic, but to "diminish" the affair of the lock of hair. This remains true in the 1714

[2] *Boileau's Lutrin: A Mock-Heroic Poem.*
[3] "The most rudimentary requisite of a mock-heroic poem is, that it should mock the epic." [Elwin-] Courthope, *E.-C.* [The Works of Pope (London, 1871–89)] v. 97.

version, in which Pope increased the length of the poem from two cantos to five (totalling 794 lines) and added such further "allusions" to the epic as the visit to the Cave of Spleen (parodying the epic visit to the underworld), the game of ombre (parodying the heroic games), the adorning of Belinda (which parallels the arming of Achilles), and above all the extensive "machinery" of Ariel and the sylphs.

That Pope should have considered the addition of further machinery is not surprising. Le Bossu had said that "the Machinery crowns the whole work," [4] while Dryden drew the conclusion that "no heroic poem can be writ on the Epicurean [i.e. atheistical] principles." [5] Pope was conversant with the formidable mass of criticism in which the function and nature of epic machinery had been discussed from the early days of the Renaissance onwards, and must have given a great deal of thought to the matter as he worked on his never-abandoned plans for an epic of his own.

In the early version of the poem Pope compromised. While supernatural agents play practically no part in the action, Lord Petre prays to Love and Jove's scales decide the issue of the battle between the beaux and belles, while the Muse, Sol, Phoebus, "Pow'rs," Winds, "the just Gods," Time and Fate, Cupid's flames, and "Heav'n" are all mentioned. Yet they are little more than rhetorical "heightening," figures of speech used to lend emphasis at important points in the action. If a more extended parody of the epic was to be attempted, machinery of a more striking sort had to be found.

One possibility would have been to revive the classical deities, peopling the Mall and Hampton Court with Pan and all his quality: another to have followed Boileau in setting personified moral qualities to preside over the action of the poem. But Pope shared Johnson's dislike of old mythology in modern poetry, and knew as well as he that "we should have turned away from a contest between Venus and Diana"; while the fact that the visit to the Cave of Spleen is the least delightful part of the poem suggests that Pope did well to decline to follow any farther the example of Boileau. It was not by modelling his machinery on Discord, Piety, and Faith and the other cold personifications of *Le Lutrin* that Pope was to make *The Rape of the Lock* the subtle masterpiece of its kind.

By a stroke of luck and of genius Pope hit on the notion of basing his machinery on the Rosicrucian spirits recently described in *Le Comte de Gabalis*. Once the idea occurred to him every thought he

[4] *A General View of the Epick Poem . . . Extracted from Bossu*, and prefixed to Pope's *Odyssey*. Sect. VII.
[5] *Essays*, II, 210.

gave to the matter must have made the choice seem the more fortunate. Since Bayle had described the Rosicrucians as "but a Sect of Mountebanks," [6] the creatures in whom they believed had about them a suggestion of the fanciful and the far-fetched which made them particularly suitable for a mock-epic. Great scope for description was given by the fact that the Rosicrucians identified their sylphs, gnomes, nymphs, and salamanders at once with the pagan deities and (with a fine catholicism) with the "Gothic" fairies of the Middle Ages. Their "Elementary Nations" combined the mischievous habits of the latter with the interest in human life characteristic of Venus and Diana. They delight—the Count tells his interlocutor—"in teaching [human beings] to live morally; [and] in giving them most wise and salutary Counsels." This enabled Pope to parody, *inter alia,* the use of "Guardian Angels" in heroic verse recommended by Dryden and practised by Cowley.

Even more important was the erotic quality of the Rosicrucian spirits. Le Bossu pointed out that "each Epick Poem has . . . some peculiar *Passion,* which distinguishes it in particular from other Epick Poems, and constitutes a kind of singular and individual difference between these Poems of the same Species. These singular Passions correspond to the *Character* of the *Hero.*" It is not surprising that as the "peculiar Passions" of the *Iliad* are *"Anger* and *Terrour* . . . because *Achilles* is angry, and the most Terrible of all Men," while "the *soft* and *tender Passions*" reign in the *Æneid,* "because that is the Character of *Æneas,*" so coquetry is the reigning passion in Pope's epic of Belinda's stolen lock. The erotic interest of *Le Comte de Gabalis* is very marked. The principal object of the Rosicrucian spirits is to carry on love-affairs with human beings, because in this way they are permitted to gain immortality. Initiates of the cult renounce mortal women[7] and take as their mistresses nymphs and sylphs, whose "Beauty is exquisite, and incomparably beyond that of the Daughters of Men." Piquancy is added by the fact that the Rosicrucian spirits, jealous as they are of mortal women, do not restrict their lovers to one member of their own elemental race.

While Pope found in the Rosicrucian doctrine many hints which he could develop, however, the supernatural agents of *The Rape of the Lock* are essentially his own creation. Whereas the emphasis

[6] *The Diverting History of the Count de Gabalis.* As the title suggests, the book was written purely to "divert." The narrator regards the Count as an amusing madman.

[7] Pope adapts the idea, and makes Ariel retire from Belinda 'amaz'd, confus'd' when she sees
> An Earthly Lover lurking at her Heart. (iii, 143–6.)

throughout *Le Comte de Gabalis* is laid on the desirability of these
spirits to men as "elementary" mistresses, in Pope's poem they figure
primarily as the allies of women in their unceasing war with mankind.
Nor did Pope find in *de Gabalis* more than the slightest hints towards
the airy beauty of his supernatural beings. The main thing that he
took over was merely the licence to invent a fantastic race whose
presence would make every trivial incident in his poem "appear of the
utmost Importance." The sylphs are mirrors added to his scene. By
them the central action is reflected and multiplied a hundredfold,
gaining in subtlety and mystery as well as in ironical importance.

The creation of the sylphs allowed Pope's imagination a much
wider scope than before. "An heroic poet is not tied to a bare representation of what is true, or exceedingly probable," Dryden had written; ". . . he may let himself loose to visionary objects, and to the
representation of such things as depending not on sense, and therefore
not to be comprehended by knowledge, may give him a freer scope for
imagination." The epic poet's task of arousing "admiration" was particularly associated with the supernatural machinery of his poem. In
the description of the sylphs and their actions Pope made his own bid
to arouse "admiration."

English poetry contains no passage of description more exquisite
than that of the sylphs in Canto II of *The Rape of the Lock.*

Of the four "Elementary Nations" Pope concentrates on the sylphs,
whose region is the air; and air is the element which informs every
line of his description:

> He summons strait his Denizens of Air;
> The lucid Squadrons round the Sails repair:
> Soft o'er the Shrouds Aerial Whispers breathe,
> That seem'd but *Zephyrs* to the Train beneath.
> Some to the Sun their Insect-Wings unfold,
> Waft on the Breeze, or sink in Clouds of Gold.
> Transparent Forms, too fine for mortal Sight,
> Their fluid Bodies half dissolv'd in Light.
> Loose to the Wind their airy Garments flew,
> Thin glitt'ring Textures of the filmy Dew. (II, 55–64)

After the aetherial beauty of these lines Pope takes up the slightest
of hints in *Le Comte de Gabalis* and describes some of the colours
which the sylphs display:

> Dipt in the richest Tincture of the Skies,
> Where Light disports in ever-mingling Dies,
> While ev'ry Beam new transient Colours flings,

> Colours that change whene'er they wave their Wings.
> Amid the Circle, on the gilded Mast,
> Superior by the Head, was *Ariel* plac'd;
> His Purple Pinions opening to the Sun,
> He rais'd his Azure Wand, and thus begun. (II, 65–72)

Such colour is only one aspect of the beauty which Pope describes. Throughout the poem the senses are flattered as delicately as they are in Belinda's world itself. It is fitting that the punishments inflicted on negligent sylphs should be the quintessence of torture of the senses. Such a sinner

> Shall feel sharp Vengeance soon o'ertake his Sins,
> Be stopt in *Vials,* or transfixt with *Pins;*
> Or plung'd in Lakes of bitter *Washes* lie,
> Or wedg'd whole Ages in a *Bodkin's* Eye:
> *Gums* and *Pomatums* shall his Flight restrain,
> While clog'd he beats his silken Wings in vain;
> Or Alom-*Stypticks* with contracting Power
> Shrink his thin Essence like a rivell'd Flower. (II, 125–32)

While the machinery gave Pope an unrivalled opportunity of indulging his descriptive powers, the descriptive passages in *The Rape of the Lock* are by no means confined to those dealing with the sylphs and their elemental colleagues. Perhaps it is because a mock-heroic poem has been thought of primarily as a satire on epic that the immense difference made by the nature of the poet's subject has often been overlooked. *Le Lutrin, The Dispensary,* and *The Rape of the Lock* are all mock-heroic poems describing a quarrel; but while Boileau and Garth describe the quarrels of lazy priests and grubby physicians, Pope is concerned with a quarrel in the *beau monde.* The nature of Pope's subject (and of his intention) leads to an immense difference between his "mock-epic" and those of Boileau and Garth.

Whereas the descriptions in *Le Lutrin* and *The Dispensary* (to which *MacFlecknoe* may be added) are characteristically of "low" scenes, a fat priest asleep or the building of a dispensary in the poorest quarter of London, the background of *The Rape of the Lock* is a brilliant one. . . . Dryden had parodied the *descriptio* of the heroic poem in this way:

> Close to the Walls which fair *Augusta* bind,
> (The fair *Augusta* much to fears inclin'd)
> An ancient fabrick rais'd t'inform the sight,
> There stood of yore, and *Barbican* it hight:

A watch Tower once, but now, so Fate ordains,
Of all the Pile an empty name remains.
From its old Ruins Brothel-houses rise,
Scenes of lewd loves, and of polluted joys. **. . . (64–71)**

Very different is the scene which Pope describes:

Close by those Meads for ever crown'd with Flow'rs,
Where *Thames* with Pride surveys his rising Tow'rs,
There stands a Structure of Majestick Frame,
Which from the neighb'ring *Hampton* takes its Name.

The descriptions in *The Rape of the Lock* are "mock-heroic" in a very different sense from those in *MacFlecknoe* and *The Dispensary*. Whereas Dryden and Garth had described ugly things with ironical elevation of style, Pope had objects of great beauty to describe. His poem is shot through with strands of silk from the fashionable world.

"If Virgil has merited such perpetual commendation for exalting his bees, by the majesty and magnificence of his diction," wrote Joseph Warton in his *Essay*, "does not Pope deserve equal praises, for the pomp and lustre of his language, on so trivial a subject?" The "pomp and lustre" of the idiom in which *The Rape of the Lock* is written is evident from the opening lines onwards:

What dire Offence from am'rous Causes springs,
What mighty Contests rise from trivial Things,
I sing . . .

One notes the inversion of the order of the words, the epithets, the use of the relatively "pompous" word "Contests," and the dignified march of the verse. A similar elevation is particularly noticeable at the end of Canto III:

What Time wou'd spare, from Steel receives its date,
And Monuments, like Men, submit to Fate!
Steel cou'd the Labour of the Gods destroy,
And strike to Dust th'Imperial Tow'rs of *Troy*;
Steel cou'd the Works of mortal Pride confound,
And hew Triumphal Arches to the Ground.
What wonder then, fair Nymph! thy Hairs shou'd feel
The conq'ring Force of unresisted Steel?

One has only to glance into the *Homer* to find a serious use of what is basically the same style:

> Refresh'd, they wait them to the bow'r of state,
> Where circled with his Peers *Atrides* sat:
> Thron'd next the King, a fair attendant brings
> The purest product of the crystal springs;
> High on a massy vase of silver mold,
> The burnish'd laver flames with solid gold:
> In solid gold the purple vintage flows,
> And on the board a second banquet rose.

The similarity of idiom between *The Rape of the Lock* and the *Homer* is nowhere more obvious than in the descriptions of the battles between the *beaux* and *belles* and between the opposing cards in the game of ombre:

> Now move to War her Sable *Matadores,*
> In Show like Leaders of the swarthy *Moors.* . . .

It is because the idiom of Pope's mock-epic differs from that of epic itself only in being more brilliant and (in an honourable sense) more "laboured" that he was able to work into the texture of his verse such numerous and successful parodies of the classical epics.

Even a heroic poem, however, was not expected to maintain the same elevation throughout. If bombast is to be avoided "the diction is to follow the images, and to take its colour from the complexion of the thoughts. Accordingly the *Odyssey* is not always cloathed in the majesty of verse proper to Tragedy, but sometimes descends into the plainer Narrative, and sometimes even to that familiar dialogue essential to Comedy." Of several passages in *The Rape of the Lock* where the style is noticeably lowered, the most obvious is the description of Sir Plume:

> (Sir *Plume,* of *Amber Snuff-box* justly vain,
> And the nice Conduct of a *clouded Cane*)
> With earnest Eyes, and round unthinking Face,
> He first the Snuff-box open'd, then the Case,
> And thus broke out—"My Lord, why, what the Devil?
> "Z—ds! damn the Lock! 'fore Gad, you must be civill
> "Plague on't! 'tis past a Jest—nay prithee, Pox!
> "Give her the Hair"—he spoke, and rapp'd his Box.

These lines remind us, by contrast, of the absence from the rest of the poem of the direct satiric "characters" so frequent in Pope's other work. In this one passage Pope lowers his style to what Gildon called "something New; Heroic Doggrel . . . but lately found out, where the Verse and the Subject agree."

But many of the speeches are among the most elevated passages in *The Rape of the Lock*. Pope told a friend that he was sketching an essay on the Oratory of Homer and Virgil; and one of the "very laborious and uncommon sort of indexes" which he appended to his translation of the *Iliad* shows the seriousness with which he regarded the ancient poets as rhetorical models. It divides Homer's speeches into classes, the Exhortatory or Deliberative, the Vituperative, the Narrative, the Pathetic, and the Sarcastic. Examples of each class are readily found in *The Rape of the Lock*.

The cumulative figures so prominent in the speeches are only one instance of the occurrence throughout *The Rape of the Lock* of the dignified "colours of rhetoric" associated with the heroic poem. In a note on the *Odyssey,* Pope observed that "sentences are not only allowable, but beautiful in Heroick Poetry, if they are introduced with propriety and without affectation." There are several instances in *The Rape of the Lock*:

> Oh thoughtless Mortals! ever blind to Fate,
> Too soon dejected, and too soon elate!
> Sudden these Honours shall be snatch'd away,
> And curs'd for ever this Victorious Day.

Such *sententiae,* which are introduced at points where there is a structural demand for increased elevation and solemnity, wittily emphasize the poet's "high seriousness" and serve (at the same time) as remarkably effective transitions. The lines which follow the description of the mischievous effect of coffee on Lord Petre, for example, do not only parody *Absalom and Achitophel*: they also serve as a hinge between that paragraph and the one which follows:

> Ah cease rash Youth! desist ere 'tis too late,
> Fear the just Gods, and think of *Scylla*'s Fate!
> Chang'd to a Bird, and sent to flit in Air,
> She dearly pays for *Nisus'* injur'd Hair!
>   *But when to Mischief Mortals bend their Will,*
>   *How soon they find fit Instruments of Ill!*
> Just then, *Clarissa* drew with tempting Grace
> A two-edg'd Weapon from her shining Case. . . .

If Pope was right when he said that "the use of pompous expression for low actions . . . is . . . the perfection of the Mock Epick," *The Rape of the Lock* passes the test with the highest honours. Periphrasis, for example, which is one of the manifestations of eighteenth-century poetic diction which has most frequently been attacked, is skilfully employed. In his translation of *Le Lutrin* Ozell had playfully elaborated Boileau's direct reference into a jocose periphrastic description of the things "in Vulgar Speech call'd NAILS." In the same spirit Pope uses "many periphrases, and uncommon appellations" for the scissors with which Lord Petre performs the rape—"two-edg'd Weapon," "little Engine," "glitt'ring *Forfex*," "fatal Engine," "Sheers," and "meeting Points."

At no point in *The Rape of the Lock* are epic methods of "heightening" merely reproduced, any more than they are merely ridiculed: they are always subtly adapted to Pope's own ends. This may be seen in the vaunting oath sworn by Lord Petre:

> While Fish in Streams, or Birds delight in Air,
> Or in a Coach and Six the *British* Fair,
> As long as *Atalantis* shall be read,
> Or the small Pillow grace a Lady's Bed,
> While *Visits* shall be paid on solemn Days,
> When numerous Wax-lights in bright Order blaze,
> While Nymphs take Treats, or Assignations give,
> So long my Honour, Name, and Praise shall live!

Pope is here using the classical formula, with a witty appropriateness, to fill in the picture of Belinda's world. The carefully selected details emphasize the artificiality of the milieu which he describes. Similarly the yoking together of ideas which normally belong to very different levels of seriousness has a strongly satirical effect:

> Sooner shall Grass in *Hide*-Park *Circus* grow,
> And Wits take Lodgings in the Sound of *Bow*;
> Sooner let Earth, Air, Sea, to *Chaos* fall,
> Men, Monkies, Lap-dogs, Parrots, perish all!

Just as it is uncertain what disaster is imminent in Canto II—

> Whether the Nymph shall break *Diana*'s Law,
> Or some frail *China* Jar receive a Flaw,
> Or stain her Honour, or her new Brocade

(an effect concisely obtained by zeugma in the line "Or lose her Heart, or Necklace, at a Ball")—so

> Not youthful Kings in Battel seiz'd alive,
> Not scornful Virgins who their Charms survive,

> Not ardent Lovers robb'd of all their Bliss,
> Not ancient Ladies when refus'd a Kiss,
> Not Tyrants fierce that unrepenting die,
> Not *Cynthia* when her *Manteau*'s pinn'd awry,
> E'er felt such Rage, Resentment and Despair,
> As Thou, sad Virgin! for thy ravish'd Hair!

Such passages, like the single line

> Puffs, Powders, Patches, Bibles, Billet-doux,

emphasize the topsy-turvy chaos of values in Belinda's world. It is the same fragile universe as that in the *Verses on the Death of Dr. Swift,* painted with more forbearance.

Unlike *MacFlecknoe, The Rape of the Lock* contains very few of the directly "diminishing" images of straightforward satire. Far more numerous are mock-heroic images which enhance the effect of the fundamental irony.

> Not fierce *Othello* in so loud a Strain
> Roar'd for the Handkerchief that caus'd his Pain

as Belinda called for the ravished lock.

> [As] Ladies in Romance assist their Knight,
> Present the Spear, and arm him for the Fight,

so Clarissa hands the fatal scissors to Lord Petre. The apotheosis of the lock is illustrated from Roman myth:

> So *Rome*'s great Founder to the Heav'ns withdrew,
> To *Proculus* alone confess'd in view.

The game of ombre is dignified by several elaborate similes (notably that which compares the scattering of the cards to the dispersal of a "routed Army"), as is the battle of the *beaux* and *belles:*

> So when bold *Homer* makes the Gods engage,
> And heav'nly Breasts with human Passions rage;
> 'Gainst *Pallas, Mars; Latona, Hermes* Arms;
> And all *Olympus* rings with loud Alarms.
> *Jove's* Thunder roars, Heav'n trembles all around;
> Blue *Neptune* storms, the bellowing Deeps resound:
> *Earth* shakes her nodding Tow'rs, the Ground gives way;
> And the pale Ghosts start at the Flash of Day!

"A game of romps was never so well dignified before."

Such are the images which one expects to find in a mock-heroic

poem. Less simple in its effect is the comparison of Belinda to the sun
at the beginning of Canto II:

> Not with more Glories, in th'Etherial Plain,
> The Sun first rises o'er the purpled Main,
> Than issuing forth, the Rival of his Beams
> Launch'd on the Bosom of the Silver *Thames*.

There is a paradox about this image which is the paradox about the
whole poem. In the simple mock-heroic, of which *MacFlecknoe* is a
good example, the subject of the poem is compared to something great
and made ridiculous by the comparison. It is "a sort of [deliberate]
transgression against the rules of proportion and mechanicks: it is
using a vast force to lift a *feather*." The comparison of Shadwell to
Hannibal is, simply, comic; and the result is denigration. The comparison of Belinda to the sun is different. It is a wild exaggeration,
hardly less absurd for being a commonplace image in love poetry; and
Pope was fully aware of its absurdity. But it is not merely absurd: it
contains an element of the same imaginative truth as the line

> *Belinda* smil'd, and all the World was gay.

What is true of the comparison of Belinda to the sun is true of the
whole conception of *The Rape of the Lock*. There is an element of
the incongruous in comparing a pretty girl to the sun and describing
her life in the style appropriate to the adventures of a hero, but it is
a different incongruity from that created by comparing Shadwell to
Hannibal and describing his "coronation" in the heroic style. While
the heroic idiom of *MacFlecknoe* merely ridicules, the heroic idiom of
The Rape of the Lock has its measure of appropriateness as well as of
inappropriateness. Eighteenth-century theorists referred to the "dignity" with which the mock-heroic treatment of a trivial subject invests
it: whereas in *MacFlecknoe* this dignity is wholly ironical, in *The Rape
of the Lock* it is not.

MacFlecknoe is a poem against Shadwell, a lampoon making no
pretensions to a moral purpose: *The Rape of the Lock* is not a poem
against anyone. In so far as it is a satire, it opposes not a person but a
moral fault: immoderate female pride. Its satire is not directed against
Arabella Fermor but against a weakness which she shares with half the
world. There is a further difference. While every line in *MacFlecknoe*
contributes to the annihilation of Shadwell, it is not true that every
line in *The Rape of the Lock* directly satirizes women's folly. Pope's
object is quite different from Dryden's. Dryden wished to laugh Shadwell out of court. Pope wishes to laugh the quarrel out of court, and
in such a way as to give serious offence to nobody. Dryden's aim is to

arouse in the reader's mind contempt for Shadwell: Pope's is to con-
ciliate everybody by means of mirth.

This peculiarity in the tone of *The Rape of the Lock* was noticed
by Dennis. "What can this Author mean," he asks angrily, "by
creating in his Readers an Expectation of Pleasantry [by describing his
poem as *Heroi-Comical*], when there is not so much as one Jest in his
Book?" What annoyed him (apart from personal dislike of Pope) was
that the reader of *The Rape of the Lock* is seldom encouraged to
throw back his head and laugh. Dennis looked for the comedy of absurd incidents exemplified by *Hudibras* and *MacFlecknoe*. Pope supplied comedy of a different sort—a subtler irony akin to the high
comedy of Molière.

The moral of *The Rape of the Lock* must not be forgotten. If he
meant to include the poem amongst the early work in which "pure
Description held the Place of Sense," Pope was being deliberately unfair. *The Rape of the Lock* is itself the best evidence that "Sense" may
be expressed by means of a "fable" and made more vivid by narrative
and description. For all his delight in the beauty of Belinda's world
Pope never allows it to arrogate the place which rightly belongs to
the sovereignty of Sense.

The full complexity of his attitude may be examined in the lines
in which "Belinda dressing is painted in as pompous a manner, as
Achilles arming":

> And now, unveil'd, the *Toilet* stands display'd,
> Each Silver Vase in mystic Order laid.
> First, rob'd in White, the Nymph intent adores
> With Head uncover'd, the *Cosmetic* Pow'rs.
> A heav'nly Image in the Glass appears,
> To that she bends, to that her Eyes she rears;
> Th'inferior Priestess, at her Altar's side,
> Trembling, begins the sacred Rites of Pride.
> Unnumber'd Treasures ope at once, and here
> The various Off'rings of the World appear;
> From each she nicely culls with curious Toil,
> And decks the Goddess with the glitt'ring Spoil.
> This Casket *India*'s glowing Gems unlocks,
> And all *Arabia* breathes from yonder Box.
> The Tortoise here and Elephant unite,
> Transform'd to *Combs*, the speckled and the white. (I, 121–36)

Pope delights in the "artificial beauty" that he is describing. Yet he
passes a judgement, which is expressed by the imagery of the whole
passage. Just as Ben Jonson makes Volpone condemn himself out of

his own mouth by apostrophizing Gold in idolatrous terms, so in the description of the toilet-table Pope shows Belinda lavishing on her own beauty the adoration which should be reserved for a higher object. Pope acknowledges the beauty of the scene, and paints it brilliantly; yet he reminds the reader that the rites he is describing are those "of *Pride.*" In the thought of the eighteenth century pride remained the first of sins. By making it "sacred" Belinda, and the whole *beau monde* which she represents, is guilty of a serious moral fault.

Pope's moral judgement is implicit throughout. Although the speeches of Piety and Hygeia in *Le Lutrin* and *The Dispensary* afforded precedents, it was hardly necessary for him to introduce Clarissa's speech, as he did in 1717, "to open more clearly the moral of the Poem."

If it had lacked a moral, explicit or implicit, *The Rape of the Lock* would have failed to meet one of the basic demands of Augustan heroic theory. Blackmore was strictly orthodox when he censured those who "look upon an heroick Poem as only a delightful Entertainment of the Imagination by beautiful Diction and surprizing Turns, and of the Understanding by a regular and well-imagined Symmetry in the Structure," and insisted that "Instruction and incitements to heroick Virtue, worthy Passions and generous Resolutions, are the principal Things aimed at in this Sort of Writing, without which a pretended Epick Poem, its chief End being destroyed, is an impertinent and lifeless Performance."

The demand for a "moral" in a heroic poem was not necessarily as pedantic as it appears to most people today. A good poem, like a good play or a good novel, is never a mere chronicle of events: it has always a meaning. When the Renaissance critic inquired what the moral of an epic was, he was posing the same question as Henry James when he asked, "What is this novel *about?*" In a deep sense the moral of a poem is its significance, the expression on the countenance of the events which it describes. Its insistence on a moral was not the least of the ways in which the theory of the mock-epic helped Pope to develop his occasional poem on a lovers' tiff until it became what Warton justly called "the best satire extant."

Am'rous Causes

by Reuben A. Brower

What dire Offence from am'rous Causes springs,
What mighty Contests rise from trivial Things . . .

We can imagine the amusement with which Pope and his fellow Scriblerians might overhear a discourse on the *Rape of the Lock* and heroic tradition. The *Key to the Lock* and the *Art of Sinking in Poetry* show what they might do with the theme—sufficient warning to any critic "who delights to trace the mind from the rudeness of its first conceptions to the elegance of its last." However much we may learn from such a study about the growth of the poem and the richness of its texture, we cannot, as Valéry reminds us, confuse the process of composition with poetic effect. For the critic, as for the common reader, the *Rape of the Lock* must be the final "elegance," the "easy art," the wit and good nature that Pope praised in Voiture:

> In these gay Thoughts the Loves and Graces shine,
> And all the Writer lives in ev'ry Line;
> His easie Art may happy Nature seem,
> Trifles themselves are Elegant in him.

The *Epistle to Miss Blount, With the Works of Voiture,* from which these lines come, and which is so close in tone and subject to the *Rape of the Lock,* was completed only a year or so before Pope wrote the first version of his "Heroi-Comical Poem."

Pope's poetry of wit in the *Rape of the Lock* is probably most perfect in the passage on the ceremony of afternoon coffee and the cutting of the lock [III, 105–54].

It is easy enough to pick out the phrases that catch the essence of the poem: "shining Altars," "glitt'ring *Forfex*," "fatal Engine," "Airy

---

"Am'rous Causes" by Reuben A. Brower. From Alexander Pope: The Poetry of Allusion *(Oxford: Clarendon Press, 1959). Copyright 1959 by the Clarendon Press, Oxford. Reprinted by permission of the author and publisher. This essay has been slightly shortened and the footnotes deleted for the purposes of this edition.*

Band." All are characteristic of the whole, and yet perfect for the occasion. What do we mean by the "poetry of wit" as illustrated by these expressions? "Glitt'ring *Forfex*," for example, sounds like an epic formula, the usual combination of epithet and noun with a flavour of mystery about its exact meaning. The use of a solemn Latin term for a familiar object, the word in which the point (!) focuses, is in Dryden's finest satirical-heroic style, but "glitt'ring," a favourite adjective in the *Rape of the Lock* and other early poems, is pure Pope. It is the adjective that makes us feel the minuteness of the actual "Forfex" and that diverts our attention to an irrelevant beauty. The Baron's heroic act seems very slight by the Homeric standard, yet exquisitely beautiful and touched somehow with the fire of that splendid world. The essence of Pope's wit in the *Rape of the Lock* lies in this beautiful diminution, where "beautiful" implies the appeal of the surface and the appeal of a better world of noble manners and actions. Cutting the lock is absurd, but also much more than absurd.

Of the phrases we have chosen, "fatal Engine" probably comes closest to the allusive irony of Dryden, with its echoes of Virgil and Milton. Dryden's *Aeneid* serves here for Virgil, the phrase being his translation of *fatalis machina*. For a moment Pope sustains the grander tone of *Absalom and Achitophel,*

> Ev'n then, before the fatal Engine clos'd . . .

but with the next line,

> A wretched *Sylph* too fondly interpos'd . . .

he restores the scale of the scene, and "the fatal Engine" is reduced to

> The little Engine on his Fingers' Ends . . .

Both phrases give us in passing a sense of the precious slightness of objects and actions. Presently, as in his *Iliad*, Pope reinforces the heroic by borrowing from Milton:

> Fate urg'd the Sheers, and cut the *Sylph* in twain,
> (But Airy Substance soon unites again) . . .

Milton's ". . . but th' Ethereal substance clos'd" is adjusted to fit Pope's more delicate myth and tone, where Dryden would easily have taken "ethereal" in his stride. "Airy," reminding us of Pope's closeness to Donne, amuses by the contrast with Milton and evokes the misty charm of Ariel and his "lucid Squadrons." In "shining Altars" there is the same witty diminution and sensuous appeal as in "glitt'ring *Forfex*," but here the visual detail fits into a scene of the heroic pictorial type familiar in Pope's *Iliad,* a description that gives an initial impression of being in Dryden's grandest epic manner. Opening with Virgilian rhetorical pomp ("For lo!"), it rises to a Latin gravity in "frequent Cups prolong the rich Repast."

But with "hover round the Fair," we hear the familiar accent of "society," and with

> *Coffee,* (which makes the Politician wise,
> And see thro' all things with his half-shut Eyes)

we are in the coffeehouse where a worldly observer is speaking to us in an aside. "Sent up in Vapours" is fashionable psychology served up as a joke. In the *Rape of the Lock* the epic grandeur is always being lightly qualified by this voice that takes us into the poet's confidence. Compared to the delicate game of innuendo that Pope plays with such consummate skill, the usual mock-epic tricks of inflation seem almost crude. Even at the climax of the action, the most heroic moment in the poem, Pope manages to insinuate this confidential tone by the lightest of touches:

> But when to Mischief Mortals bend their Will,
> How soon they find fit Instruments of Ill!

The couplet, as the notes remind us, is indebted to *Henry VI* and to *Absalom and Achitophel.* But,

> Just then, *Clarissa* drew with tempting Grace
> A two-edg'd Weapon from her shining Case . . .

"Just then" (the transition in a children's story), and a little later, "just behind" (the feminine accent of "just *there,* my dear"), incline the tone towards cosy intimacy. Dryden's manner is by comparison elephantine.

Yet Pope's *"Spectator"* tone, as Sherburn calls it, makes possible a personal moral seriousness rare in Dryden (to speak in these terms may be worse than elephantine). In the present passage the tone allows Pope to move out from "coffee" to a sharp criticism of statesmanship. Although in recent years too much has been said too solemnly about Pope's serious concerns in the *Rape of the Lock,* it would be light-minded to disregard them. In the better "case" implied by Pope's satire, marriage is not entered into lightly or unadvisedly, the ceremony of innocence is not drowned, and beauty in nature and in art are truly wonderful. But the chief moral, like all poetic "morals," is inseparable from the poetry, from Pope's peculiar wit and tone:

> What then remains, but well our Pow'r to use,
> And keep good Humour still whate'er we lose?
> And trust me, Dear! good Humour can prevail,
> When Airs, and Flights, and Screams, and Scolding fail.
> Beauties in vain their pretty Eyes may roll;
> Charms strike the Sight, but Merit wins the Soul. (v. 29–34)

In a Dedication that is a perfect example of the virtue he recommends, Pope says to the original Belinda,

> It will be in vain to deny that I have some Regard for this Piece, since I Dedicate it to You. Yet You may bear me Witness, it was intended only to divert a few young Ladies, who have good Sense and good Humour enough, to laugh not only at their Sex's little unguarded Follies, but at their own.

Through poetic laughter Pope is everywhere urging his readers to view these "Follies" with the necessary distance, moral and aesthetic. He wins us over to mature "Good Sense and good Humour" by the art of allusive irony that he had originally learned from Dryden and that he now adapts to suit his own aims and sensibility. He gets his purchase on his larger meanings by skilful handling of various literary traditions, Ovidian, pastoral, and heroic. Pope's keen responsiveness to the society about him is expressed through an equally keen responsiveness to literary modes that had imaged other societies, both human and divine.

While it is true that in its general conception the *Rape of the Lock* derives from the *Battle of the Frogs and Mice,* from Tassoni, and more immediately from Boileau and Garth, the actual style of the poem shows rather how much Pope owed to the tradition of Dryden and how much he still was learning from the first of the Augustans. In details of language, as nearly every page of the Twickenham Edition shows, Pope borrows more often from Dryden than from any other single poet. Even when he is not borrowing directly, he is indebted to the late seventeenth-century heroic style that Dryden had fixed as proper for epic and mock-epic.

From early in his career we see Pope imitating Dryden, and yet imparting his own quality to his imitations. The two manners dominant in the older poet, the style of public address and the heroic, have left traces on Pope's earliest poems. Pope had seen Dryden once, and in his uneasy friendship with Wycherley he enjoyed a repeat performance of Restoration literary life in its less elegant form. His first attempt in satire, *To the Author of a Poem, intitled, Successio* (Settle), has the hearty coarseness and the free-and-easy classical comparisons

of Dryden's less finished prologues, while the lines *On Dulness* and
other additions to Wycherley's poems resemble the heavier attacks on
Shadwell in *Absalom and Achitophel*, Part II. The comparison of
dullness with "the Leaden Byass of a Bowl," patterned on the "bias
of the mind" simile in *MacFlecknoe*, was to find a place in the
Dunciad, the nearest to Dryden of all Pope's major works. But a lightness and grace of rhythm more characteristic of Pope can be felt in
some of these fragments, especially in the *"Similitude"* on "the Stream
of Life." Note that Pope's rhythm comes out more distinctly in the
lines after the triplet (in itself characteristic of Dryden):

> The Stream of Life shou'd more securely flow
> In constant Motion, nor too swift nor slow,
> And neither swell too high, nor sink too low;
> Not always glide thro' gloomy Vales, and rove
> ('Midst Flocks and Shepherds) in the silent Grove;
> But more diffusive in its wand'ring Race;
> Serve peopled Towns, and Stately Cities grace;
> Around in sweet Meanders wildly range,
> Kept fresh by Motion, and unchang'd by Change. (18–26)

Though these are the lines of a town poet, there is a marked similarity
in idiom and descriptive style to the "retirement" passage in *Windsor
Forest* (ll. 235–70). We have already glanced at early experiments in
the heroic style such as the *Episode of Sarpedon* and the *Gardens of
Alcinous*, which in their choice pictorial details and smoother, more
evenly balanced couplets, show a sensibility quite different from
Dryden's.

The *Ode for Musick on St. Cecilia's Day*, though painfully imita-
tive of Dryden, has one passage that anticipates the romantic mythological style of Collins and the early Keats:

> By the Streams that ever flow,
> By the fragrant Winds that blow
>   O'er th' *Elysian* Flowers,
> By those happy Souls who dwell
> In Yellow Meads of *Asphodel,*
>   Or *Amaranthine* Bowers:
> By the Heroe's armed Shades,
> Glitt'ring thro' the gloomy Glades,
> By the Youths that dy'd for Love,
> Wandring in the Myrtle Grove,
>   Restore, restore *Eurydice* to Life . . . (71–81)

The blend of heroic reminiscence with delicate imagery, the classical elegance of diction and movement, are what we should expect from the future poet of the *Rape of the Lock*. These qualities are combined with Pope's intimacy of address (his *Spectator* tone) in the close of the *Epistle to Miss Blount, With the Works of Voiture,* lines that might have been written to Belinda:

> Now crown'd with Myrtle, on th' *Elysian* Coast,
> Amid those Lovers, joys his gentle Ghost,
> Pleas'd while with Smiles his happy Lines you view,
> And finds a fairer *Ramboüillet* in you.
> The brightest Eyes of *France* inspir'd his Muse,
> The brightest Eyes of *Britain* now peruse,
> And dead as living, 'tis our Author's Pride,
> Still to charm those who charm the World beside. (73–80)

The epistle is a miniature exhibition of what Pope can do at this point in his career and of what he will do in the *Rape of the Lock* and in a number of his later satires. In the urbanity of Voiture's art and personal life he sees an ideal for himself, which he expresses with a lightness and sureness of rhythm that beautifully symbolize an easy inner poise:

> Thus wisely careless, innocently gay,
> Chearful, he play'd the Trifle, Life, away,
> 'Till Fate scarce felt his gentle Breath supprest,
> As smiling Infants sport themselves to Rest . . . (11–14)

Pope offers the lady this image of freedom in contrast with the formal restraint of custom and a "successful" marriage. Although he is charmed by feminine beauty, he sees through the glitter with the eye of the later satirist and harshly brings out the uglinesss glimpsed "thro' half-shut eyes" in the *Rape of the Lock*. The lady is offered the same consolation and defence in both poems:

> Trust not too much your now resistless Charms,
> Those, Age or Sickness, soon or late, disarms;
> *Good Humour* only teaches Charms to last,
> Still makes new Conquests, and maintains the past . . . (59–62)

In the mastery of a personal attitude and of a corresponding intimacy of tone and ease of rhythm, Pope sets himself apart from Dryden while continuing to write within the mode of Dryden's finest epistolary poems such as the prologue *To my Dear Friend Mr. Congreve* or the epistle *To Sir Godfrey Kneller.*

It was characteristic of Pope and of his integrity as a poet that the traditional styles with which he had been experimenting should find a place in the work that most surely marks his arrival at maturity. We have seen how he renewed his early pastoral style in the scene of Belinda's journey down the Thames, how he parodied the style without burlesquing it, expressing in this way an awareness of a world where man had once lived in significant and harmonious relationship with Nature. It is not unexpected that his youthful experiments with Ovid also left a mark on the *Rape of the Lock*. In making his versions of the *Metamorphoses* Pope had again been imitating Dryden, and in particular the heroic style of his translations from Ovid. As a result Pope's *Fables* are closer to the heroic than to the implied tone of easy colloquial speech of the original, although his *Vertumnus and Pomona* has a more Ovidian lightness of touch than his *Dryope*. But whatever their failings as translations, they gave Pope valuable experience in combining gallantry and heroics in narratives of magical change. Partly owing to this early practice the *Rape of the Lock* is epic "Ovidianized." There are the specific borrowings such as the change of the lock into a star, the allusion to Scilla's theft of Nisus' sacred lock, and the comparison of Sir Fopling's death to "th' expiring Swan" of *Dido to Aeneas*. (All are discussed in Tillotson's excellent introduction.) But more important proof of Ovid's influence is the total effect of Ovidian transformation, of an imagined region where belles become nymphs and goddesses, playing cards become Homeric heroes, and where the whims and concealed passions of lovers are turned into creatures of the four elements. Significantly enough, Ariel comes from the *Tempest*, the Shakespearean play that is most thoroughly permeated by Ovidian metamorphosis. In its union of the comedy of young love with classical myth and fairy lore, the *Rape of the Lock* stands as Pope's *Midsummer Night's Dream*, the last successful work in the Renaissance mythological tradition that includes the tales of Marlowe, Lodge, and Drayton, and the plays of Lyly. Pope's success in this mode, like the Elizabethans', depends less on learning than on a happy gift of mythological invention. As Tillotson finely notes, Pope is being thoroughly Ovidian when he sees among the wonders of the dressing table,

> The Tortoise here and Elephant unite,
> Transform'd to *Combs,* the speckled and the white. (I. 135–6)

And where is there a better piece of mythological "seeing" than in the vision of the sylphs, in which the human and the natural interchange with all the fluidity of metamorphosis?

> He summons strait his Denizens of Air;
> The lucid Squadrons round the Sails repair:
> Soft o'er the Shrouds Aerial Whispers breathe,
> That seem'd but *Zephyrs* to the Train beneath.
> Some to the Sun their Insect-Wings unfold,
> Waft on the Breeze, or sink in Clouds of Gold.
> Transparent Forms, too fine for mortal Sight,
> 'Their fluid Bodies half dissolv'd in Light.
> Loose to the Wind their airy Garments flew,
> Thin glitt'ring Textures of the filmy Dew;
> Dipt in the richest Tincture of the Skies,
> Where Light disports in ever-mingling Dies,
> While ev'ry Beam new transient Colours flings,
> Colours that change whene'er they wave their Wings. (II. 55–68)

The sylphs and the heroic actors of the *Rape of the Lock* are Ovidian in still another way that links Pope's invention with the *Metamorphoses*. In his epic of transformations Ovid shocks and amuses by giving divine and heroic lovers the manners and attitudes of contemporary Roman society. Although Ovid knows what real passion is, the talk of love among his heroes and divinities is full of coquetry and extremely "wise." In similar fashion Pope's spirits are "Denizens of Air" and of London society, unsubstantial, but very knowing in all the arts of love. Their view of beauty is reminiscent of Ovid's *Ars Amatoria*:

> Our humbler Province is to tend the Fair,
> Not a less pleasing, tho' less glorious Care.
> To save the Powder from too rude a Gale,
> Nor let th' imprison'd Essences exhale,
> To draw fresh Colours from the vernal Flow'rs,
> To steal from Rainbows ere they drop in Show'rs
> A brighter Wash; to curl their waving Hairs,
> Assist their Blushes, and inspire their Airs;
> Nay oft, in Dreams, Invention we bestow,
> To change a *Flounce,* or add a *Furbelo*. (II. 91–100)

Belinda's charms are the product of magical cosmetic arts over which the "busy *Sylphs*" preside,

> And *Betty*'s prais'd for Labours not her own. (I. 148)

Pope's refashioning of epic in Ovidian terms, making it more splendid and more amusing, is one of the large ways in which he adapted heroic poetry to his purposes in the *Rape of the Lock*.

But Pope was thoroughly aware that he was writing in an established genre practised by many poets before him. Besides being familiar with well-known examples of mock-heroic and burlesque poetry, he also must have read Dryden's comments on the relations between satire and heroic poetry, and he was certainly well acquainted with contemporary theories of the epic. More important, he had first-hand knowledge of Homer, Virgil, and the English "heroic" poets. The 1713 revision of the *Rape of the Lock*, in which the epic machinery was added, was made at the time when Scriblerus Club was in full swing, in an atmosphere of mockery of solemn learning and literature of all kinds. Earlier in the same year Pope had published his ironic essay on pastoral poetry and his prose burlesque, *A Receit to make an Epick Poem*. The proposals for the *Iliad* had gone out in 1713, and by May of 1714 he was surely at work on the translation. He may have already started to translate before completing the revision of the *Rape of the Lock* in December 1713. The resemblances between the poem and the translation of the *Iliad* are at points very close, but . . . it is impossible to decide whether Pope is parodying his translation or anticipating it. In a broad sense, Pope had always been a translator of Homer, from his early experiments in epic and his translations of passages from the *Iliad* and the *Odyssey*, to the *Rape of the Lock*, and the style of his *Iliad* is hardly distinguishable from that of the considerably earlier *Episode of Sarpedon* and the *Gardens of Alcinous*. Whether or not he had completed any part of the translation before revising the *Rape of the Lock*, the poem is the inevitable example for comparing Pope's heroic and mock-heroic modes.

We have already seen how finely Pope transformed heroic poetry by the beautiful diminution of phrases like "glitt'ring *Forfex*" and "shining Altars." In general he produces epic effects in the *Rape of the Lock* much as in his translation. Allusive imitation of Virgil or Dryden or Milton is the basis of his heroic style whether he is making a serious translation or writing a parody, and sharpening of visual details is as common in the epithets and scenes of the *Rape of the Lock* as of the *Iliad*. Pope's treatment of the fixed epithet in the *Rape of the Lock* makes clear what happened when he transferred the heroic style to a less serious subject. Exact translations of Homeric or Virgilian expressions are rare, though we do find "seven-fold fence" for *"sevenfold* shield" and "Garbs *succinct*" for Virgil's *succinctus,* and a fair number of phrases modelled closely on Virgil or Dryden, such as "th' Etherial Plain," "the Purpled Main," "th' Aerial Kind," "the wintry Main," and "the kindly Rain." By their generalized form and meaning, they give a passing if humorous glance at the great order of Nature "out there," beyond the doings of Belinda and her friends. "The gen'ral Fate," like similar phrases in Pope's *Iliad*, conceals the Homeric Moira under Roman solemnity and abstraction. Some of the combinations of epithet and noun—"th' Etherial Plain," "th' Aerial Kind," "the Finny Prey"—have a peculiar quality that makes them perfect for the *Rape of the Lock*. Like certain periphrases in Homer or in Virgil, especially as Englished by Dryden, they are tiny enigmas, some of them almost seventeenth-century scientific jokes, with an allusion to classification by genus and species. The definition of periphrase in the *Art of Sinking* fits precisely both the serious and the comic epic:

> *Periphrase* is another great Aid to *Prolixity*; being a diffus'd circumlocutory Manner of expressing a known Idea, which should be so misteriously couch'd, as to give the Reader the Pleasure of guessing what it is that the Author can possibly mean; and a Surprize when he finds it.

The wit latent in Virgil and apparent in Dryden (as in *volubile buxum*, "wooden engine," for a top) works with a new force in the context of the *Rape of the Lock*, since the slightly enigmatic flavour and our "Pleasure of guessing" and finding what "the Author can possibly mean" are now thoroughly in place.

The use of heroic diction for ridicule might be described simply as bad translation of the kind Pope refers to in the Preface to the *Iliad*. Render literally an epithet like "ox-eyed Hera" and set it down mechanically in any context however serious, and in English the result is absurd. (Literal translation of formulas will always seem comic to readers unfamiliar with the conventions of oral epic.) Applying in reverse his principle that the translator should use those phrases that "agree with the tenor and main intent of the particular passage," Pope gets the desired effect in the *Rape of the Lock*. Part of the fun comes from seeing Pope deliberately use clichés of the type called "diminishing Figures" in the *Art of Sinking*:

THE EXPLETIVE,

admirably exemplified in the Epithets of many Authors.

> *Th' umbrageous Shadow, and the verdant Green,*
> *The running Current, and odorous Fragrance,*
> *Chear my lone Solitude with joyous Gladness.*

But the effect of even the most commonplace eighteenth-century epithets is often more than comic. When used of the card table at Hampton Court, "verdant Field," "velvet plain," and "level Green" have their sensuous value renewed, and unexpectedly fresh images come to mind. (The silken surface becomes the smooth and shimmering expanse of an English lawn. We may note again the fine imaginative extensions of the technique in "glitt'ring Forfex" and similar phrases.) In these expressions and in many others the nice incongruity and the slightly enigmatic quality of epic language blend with lively sense impressions of scene, persons, and artifacts.

In the *Rape of the Lock,* as in the *Iliad* and the *Odyssey,* there is much poetry of luxury and well-made things, of "glitt'ring Spoil," "rich Brocade" and "silver Lamps," of "rich *China* Vessels" and "gilded Chariots." Through many descriptive devices Pope builds up little scenes of "historic painting" that are the exact complement to the grander pictures of his *Iliad.* But the art and the artist in the epullion and the epic are the same, and positive effects of magnificence and pictorial beauty persist in the *Rape of the Lock* where they "ought not to." If we refer to the effects as "exquisite," or "charming" or "Watteauesque," we also want to add something stronger. For through his use of epic style, at once traditional and highly individual, Pope realizes more serious meanings. If comparisons with battles, feasts, and sacrifices diminish the importance of the persons and events, they also express values of a world where greatness and ceremony were serious matters, where grace and beauty of manners were an index to civilization, a world alive in the "historical present" of the mind of the poet and of readers who have a sense of the past.

Probably the largest single way in which Pope imparted qualities of splendour and wonder to his actors and action was through his brilliant adaptation of epic machinery. His success in producing the "marvellous" needs little comment. Like Homer's gods, Pope's sylphs move easily in and out of the lower world, they surprise without offending our sense of the probable, and they give ordinary human impulses a sensuous form that makes us see them as they are, and yet as beautiful. What they "really" stand for—feminine honour, flirtation, courtship, the necessary rivalry of man and woman—is seen in its essence, and a human impulse seen in its essence, as Keats observed of a street quarrel, is beautiful.

By inventing the sylphs Pope solved the almost impossible problem that the theorists set for the heroic poet. He is almost certainly the only modern poet to create a company of believable deities which are not simply the ancient classical divinities in modern dress, and which are not offensive to a Christian audience. As Warburton pronounced with his usual sententiousness:

> . . . that sort of Machinery which his judgment taught him was only fit for his use, his admirable invention supplied. There was but one System in all nature which was to his purpose, the *Rosicrucian Philosophy.*

The tact with which Pope combined hints from *Rosicrucian Philosophy* with memories of Shakespeare, Milton, Lucretius, Ovid, and English country lore is finely described by Tillotson in his essay on the *Sylphs.* . . . We may also add that it was Pope's familiarity with Ovid that helped him reach a unifying vision and metaphor (the sense of magical change), and that gave him hints for creating a style in which the marvellous, the socially sophisticated, and the heroic could be successfully combined.

Pope's achievement in introducing the marvellous into a modern poem carried him well beyond mere "correctness," since he succeeded also in recovering something of Homer's vision of a human drama played in relation to a divine order. (To describe this feat without sinking in prose, we should need Pope's lightness of touch in poetry.) By deftly linking his invented deities with popular country beliefs and with the "Heathen Mythology" of Fate and Jove, Pope makes us feel the presence of forces greater than Belinda and the Baron and their friends. The dwarfing of the persons, which everyone notices, is one sign that this is so. As unchanging Nature-Moira was implied in the diction and rhythm of Pope's *Iliad,* so in the *Rape of the Lock* a larger natural order is implied through setting or descriptive epithet and playful allusion. In the "silver Thames" and the "morning Sun," in "the Rival of his Beams," and the "Nymph" with her "destructive" powers, we feel a link between social and natural worlds, and in the movement of stars and of time, we have an almost Homeric sense of the necessary end of Belinda's beauty and virtue:

> Then cease, bright Nymph! to mourn thy ravish'd Hair
> Which adds new Glory to the shining Sphere!
> Not all the Tresses that fair Head can boast
> Shall draw such Envy as the Lock you lost.
> For, after all the Murders of your Eye,
> When, after Millions slain, your self shall die;
> When those fair Suns shall sett, as sett they must,
> And all those Tresses shall be laid in Dust;
> *This Lock,* the Muse shall consecrate to Fame,
> And mid'st the Stars inscribe *Belinda*'s Name! (v. 141–50)

This is of course elegant spoofing, literary and social. We are amused by the absurdity of the apotheosis and the analogies to Daphnis (Caesar) and to Achilles lying "in the Dust," and also by the allusion to the *Lock of Berenice,* which was itself a spoof. (The effect is a kind of double parody.) We are also reminded of the *Elegy to the Memory of an Unfortunate Lady:*

> How lov'd, how honour'd once, avails thee not,
> To whom related, or by whom begot;
> A heap of dust alone remains of thee;
> 'Tis all thou art, and all the proud shall be! (71–74)

But in the *Rape of the Lock* as in the *Elegy* the death of innocence and beauty are not laughing matters, and the apotheosis offers serious as well as playful consolation to Belinda and Mrs. Arabella Fermor. With perfect deference to fact and poetic fiction, Pope has found his equivalent for Homer's Death and Sleep, and it is hard not to suppose that his sensibility and the internal form of his poem have been subtly shaped by his familiarity with the Homeric use of myth. Not only the mock apotheosis and the sylphs, but the whole drama of the *Rape of the Lock* is a piece of wonderful myth-making. "Mythos" as a fable or plot and "mythos" as symbol are two growths of the basic process of seeing and dramatizing that we first observed in the *Pastorals*. Pope's growth as a poet may be seen in his progress from the pictorial mythologizing of the *Pastorals* to the descriptive splendours and the fully developed symbolism of *Windsor Forest,* to the "fable" of Belinda's lock. In the dramatic image of the *Rape of the Lock* Pope created a native Augustan myth, as later readers have instinctively and perhaps naïvely demonstrated, by taking the poem for the stock symbol of the "Age of Queen Anne." A not wholly adequate symbol, to be sure, if we think of the public grandeurs and the common miseries of London life in 1714. For the one, we need something like the Roman-Augustan myth of *Windsor Forest*; for the other, *The Harlot's Progress* or *Beer Street* and *Gin Lane,* But Pope gives at least a hint of the grandeur in

> Where *Thames* with Pride surveys his rising Tow'rs . . . (III. 2)

and of the misery in

> . . . Wretches hang that Jury-men may Dine . . . (III. 22)

Note that both references are made through epic allusion, that Pope has found in mock-epic a way like Homer's of "looking out" on another world beyond the scene of his action. Pope uses allusion or parody to give us a glimpse of the great Homeric world, thus imitating Homer's technique while reversing the direction of our view. Similes compare Belinda with Aeneas,

> Not half so fixt the Trojan cou'd remain, (v. 5)

or the fracas over the lock with the quarrels on Olympus,

> So when bold *Homer* makes the Gods engage . . . (v. 45)

It was between these two heroic comparisons that Pope in 1717 set his *"parody of the speech of Sarpedon to Glaucus"* in order to *"open more clearly the moral of the Poem."*

> Then grave *Clarissa* graceful wav'd her Fan;
> Silence ensu'd, and thus the Nymph began.
>   Say, why are Beauties prais'd and honour'd most,
> The wise Man's Passion, and the vain Man's Toast?
> Why deck'd with all that Land and Sea afford,
> Why Angels call'd, and Angel-like ador'd?
> Why round our Coaches crowd the white-glov'd Beaus,
> Why bows the Side-box from its inmost Rows?
> How vain are all these Glories, all our Pains,
> Unless good Sense preserve what Beauty gains:
> That Men may say, when we the Front-box grace,
> Behold the first in Virtue, as in Face!
> Oh! if to dance all Night, and dress all Day,
> Charm'd the Small-pox, or chas'd old Age away;
> Who would not scorn what Huswife's Cares produce,
> Or who would learn one earthly Thing of Use?
> To patch, nay ogle, might become a Saint,
> Nor could it sure be such a Sin to paint.
> But since, alas! frail Beauty must decay,
> Curl'd or uncurl'd, since Locks will turn to grey,
> Since painted, or not painted, all shall fade,
> And she who scorns a man, must die a Maid;
> What then remains, but well our Pow'r to use,
> And keep good Humour still whate'er we lose?
> And trust me, Dear! good Humour can prevail,
> When Airs, and Flights, and Screams, and Scolding fail.
> Beauties in vain their pretty Eyes may roll;
> Charms strike the Sight, but Merit wins the Soul.
>   So spoke the Dame, but no Applause ensu'd . . . (v. 7-35)

Pope's treatment of the passage shows finally and clearly where the mock-epic of the *Rape of the Lock* stands in relation to Homer and the English heroic tradition. The main effect of Clarissa's speech for readers not over-conscious of Homer or Le Bossu comes from hearing the voice of common sense in the midst of much ado about nothing. We feel too a fairly hearty amusement in the obvious parallels to the *Iliad* and a flicker of Walleresque sentiment,

> But since, alas! frail Beauty must decay . . .

An eighteenth-century reader would recognize that Pope was now

giving "the moral" demanded by theorists and so anticipating the
objections of Dennis, who had found Pope's purpose not sufficiently
clear. Closer comparison with Homer will show how skilful parody
readjusted Homer's moral to fit the values of Augustan society.

The parody opens on Dryden's high-heroic level, with an allusion
to one of the most serious speeches in *Absalom and Achitophel,* the
"temptation" of Monmouth:

> Say, why are Beauties prais'd and honour'd most,
> The wise Man's Passion, and the vain Man's Toast?

In the Homeric counterpart, Sarpedon cites as proofs of glory the
simple goods of meat and drink, speaking of them with complete cer-
tainty as to their value. In Pope's version, as we noted in the last
chapter, Sarpedon acknowledges these glories, but they have been
raised to a nobler pitch, since they are signs of a divine blessing. The
ultimate value is "above," not here below. The translation in effect
if not in fact anticipates Clarissa's attitude. In her appeal "these
Glories" of social success are in themselves "vain," and the Homeric
parallels underline the gap between true and false grandeur. But the
superior virtue recommended by Clarissa, the combination of "good
Sense" and "good Humour," is not quite transcendental and so altogether perfect for the occasion. It is a real virtue, but a "smiling" one,
and attainable within the limits of a worldly society more inclined
to trust intelligence than enthusiasm. But it can accomplish some
fairly wonderful things:

> Charms strike the Sight, but Merit wins the Soul.

As elsewhere in the poem, Pope attunes his moral sentiments to the
mock-heroic by means of his tone,

> And trust me, Dear! good Humour can prevail,
> When Airs, and Flights, and Screams, and Scolding fail.

This is cosily feminine to the point of caricature: Clarissa moralizing
is very much "like a woman."

But in adopting such a tone Pope is edging away from mock-heroic
toward burlesque, and at some points in the passage he slips into the
kind of "jest," as Dryden would say, that "gives us a boyish kind of
pleasure." In serious neoclassical parody ordinary persons and actions
are presented in a style so nicely simulating the heroic as to barely
break the epic decorum. (This is Dryden's manner at its best in his
heroic satires.) In burlesque, by contrast, high-heroic persons are
presented in a low style, a travesty of the heroic. We take "a boyish
kind of pleasure," in seeing the style debased, and we laugh less at

the person than the language. By Canto V of the *Rape of the Lock* "grave Clarissa," Belinda, and Thalestris have become surprisingly heroic, hence any descent seems more of a let-down. Set certain lines in the passage beside Homer or beside Pope's translation, and they become in an eighteenth-century sense "vulgar":

> Oh! if to dance all Night, and dress all Day,
> Charm'd the Small-pox, or chas'd old Age away . . .
> To patch, nay ogle, might become a Saint . . .
> Curl'd or uncurl'd, since Locks will turn to grey,
> Since painted, or not painted, all shall fade . . .

The level of the diction comes perilously near to Swift's *Corinna* or *The Progress of Beauty*. Dryden will go this far in ridiculing the most despicable butts of his satire, but not often, and his best parodies of Virgil have a Latin finesse rarely equalled by Pope (probably because he was a better Latinist). Pope shows a similar finesse in parodying English poets, including Dryden himself, but his occasional coarseness has a value. By this mention of a horrid disease and the gross deceptions of cosmetics, the ugly realities of the London world are particularized and brought home to us. As a result Pope comes closer to Homer's "ten thousand shapes of death" in this burlesque than in the bland abstractions of his translation. The effect is like Gay's in *The Shepherd's Week*, where Gay recovered some of the healthy charm of Theocritus by introducing exact if vulgar details. Pope's thrust into realism in this speech and at other points in the *Rape of the Lock* brings his trifle nearer to the "naïve" realism and the inclusiveness of vision of Homeric poetry.

That some coarsening of mockery appears in a passage added in the 1717 edition is significant. Pope is no longer quite the "gayest valetudinaire alive" of his *Farewell to London*, nor the would-be Voiture of his *Epistle to Miss Blount*. He has been through his ugly experience with Curll, and he has suffered more "contamination" through various Scriblerian projects and his collaboration with Gay in the *What D'Ye Call It*, a burlesque of Addison's *Cato*. He is nearer in mood to Swift now that Swift is no longer near at hand. But he is not ready for a poem combining this vein of harshness and tougher wit with the surface magnificence of Dryden's heroic style; that is, he is not yet the poet of the *Dunciad*.

For the *Rape of the Lock* and the world Pope is mocking in the poem, consistent use of Dryden's tone would of course be absurd. It was justified in Dryden's own satires because his victims were elevated by the great public issues in which they were involved. But Pope at this point in his career has no scene or historic vision of similar scope.

His social scene, in comparison with Dryden's, is private, and the vices ridiculed and the moral offered belong to private life. But the more intimate scene favoured Pope's use of the more personal tone denied to Dryden, and though Pope can allude to the high heroic manner for ridicule or serious placing of his action, he is not bound by it, as he was in translating the *Iliad*. In his translation Pope writes within the limits of proper heroic solemnity, and he cannot allow his Jove and Juno to come down to the comic level of Zeus and Hera. If he had done so, the "true Heroick" artifice would have collapsed. But in the *Rape of the Lock,* starting from a premise of mockery, Pope is happily free to include ugly and serious implications in a literary and social *divertimento.* Pope, like Horace, can be convincingly serious only when it is certain that no one will take him quite seriously.

The Limits of Allusion in
The Rape of the Lock

by Earl R. Wasserman

The works of Pope are not likely any longer to be read as "the poetry of statement": we have become too sensible of their extraordinary subtleties at the level of language and of the wealth of their allusiveness, especially to the classics, the Bible, and the commonplaces. But although we are no longer inclined to reduce this poetry to versified statement, the vestige of that critical conception has possibly deterred admission of the full complexity of Pope's art. Disinherited as we are from his referential systems it is reasonable to question whether we are adequately aware of the scope of his allusions and their part in constituting the fabric of his poems. Hence, the ultimate question at issue here will be whether only the text of Pope's allusion acts upon his poem or whether it also imports its own context. If the context is indeed relevant, what are the permissible limits in our bringing that context to bear? How allusive are Pope's allusions? and how functional. Take the case of *The Rape of the Lock*.

Even superficial acquaintance with the classical epic will inform us of its role in shaping Pope's mock epic. The epic proposition and invocation, the adaptation of the epic battles and feasts, the Rosicrucian divine machinery, the epic style and phrasal formulas are all obvious enough; and even the function of casting Clarissa's speech in the pattern of Sarpedon's famous commentary on the hero's *raison d'être* has been made familiar to us. But perhaps Pope's reader is no longer sufficiently conscious of how deeply embedded the Latinate manner is even in his language. The Twickenham edition may have taught us that the *Aeneid* (II, 390–91) is being echoed when the Baron plans

"The Limits of Allusion in The Rape of the Lock*"* by Earl R. Wasserman, *425–444. From* Journal of English and Germanic Philology, *LXV, (1966). Reprinted by permission of the author and publisher. Most of the footnotes have been removed for the purposes of this edition.*

> By Force to ravish, or by Fraud betray;
> For when Success a Lover's Toil attends,
> Few ask, if Fraud or Force attain'd his Ends; (II, 32–34)

that Belinda's visionary beau "said, or seem'd to say" (I, 26) because these are also Virgil's words on an analogous occasion (*Aeneid*, VI, 454); and that

> Where Wigs with Wigs, with Sword-knots Sword-knots strive,
> Beaus banish Beaus, and Coaches Coaches drive (I, 101–102)

repeats a popular classical phrasal pattern. But, with our loss of Latin, it is less apparent that when Pope described the beaux and belles passing the hours "In various Talk" (III, 11) his mind instinctively reached out to the phrase *vario sermone* with which Virgil described how Aeneas and Evander lightened the tedium of their stroll (*Aeneid*, VIII, 309); or that Ovid, wittiest of the Roman poets, instructed Pope in shaping one of his most famous instances of zeugma,

> Here Thou, great *Anna*! whom three Realms obey,
> Dost sometimes Counsel take—and sometimes *Tea*. (III, 7–8)

Nor are we likely to sense that "fatal Engine" (III, 149) and "Voices strike the Skies" (V, 42) are Virgilian phrases; or that "sacrilegious Hands" (especially in the sense in which it is used in the poem, IV, 174, referring to theft of a sacred object), "Nourish'd . . . Locks" (II, 20), "Thirst of Fame" (III, 25), "painted Vessel" (II, 47), "Fate urg'd" (III, 151), and "decks . . . with the glitt'ring Spoil" (I, 132) are recurrent Latinisms. Of course the entire poem is a tissue of such classical echoes, many far more pointed and palpable than these; and the phrases mentioned are not allusive in any significant sense. But, by indicating how radical Latin is even in Pope's language, they serve to tell us that the mind that composed *The Rape of the Lock* was less an English one hearkening back to the classics for witty references than one applying itself to an English social situation from the viewpoint of a deeply ingrained classicism. Classical literature and its manners, together with Scripture and its exegetical tradition, are not merely Pope's acquired learning; they shaped the character and processes of his thought. Correspondingly, his poems consistently ask for a reader who is equally native to the whole classical-Scriptural world, a Christian Greco-Roman scrutinizing eighteenth-century English culture. On that assumption I propose to survey the poem in order to observe what may be the consequences of setting various passages in the contexts they evoke.

Before doing so in any systematic way, however, I should like to examine a parenthetical passage in the poem which illustrates the kind of ready knowledge Pope demands of his reader and which also can serve as a paradigm of the significant interactions taking place between his text and the allusion it calls up. The time at which Belinda undertakes the contest at Ombre is set by the poet as the hour when

> The hungry Judges soon the Sentence sign,
> And Wretches hang that Jury-men may Dine;
> The Merchant from th'*Exchange* returns in Peace,
> And the long Labours of the *Toilette* cease. (III, 21–24)

Elsewhere the poet, striking a Beau Brummel pose, equivocates between Belinda's world of social elegance and the matter-of-fact world that encompasses it—the Queen's taking counsel and taking tea, the foredooming of "Foreign Tyrants" and domestic tyrants ("Nymphs at home")—until he has made a charming mockery of the distinction between serious necessity and frivolous artifice. But in the context of the sheltered Petit Trianon world of conventionalized manners that the total poem constructs, the lines on the judges and the merchant are, as it were, the poet's one hard glance at the Hobbesian state of nature raging outside, so that he may expose the ugly alternative for Belinda and her friends if they shatter the fragile decorum that fences them in. In addition, Pope expects his ideal reader to recognize the Homeric character of the two couplets if they are to have their full force. In a note to a line in the *Dunciad* he wrote, "This is to mark punctually the Time of the day: *Homer* does it by the circumstances of the Judges rising from court, or of the Labourer's dinner" (A II, 258 n.); and this suggests that Homer's two methods are expected to be known and that Pope's reader is to recognize in the quoted couplets the conjunction of both of these Homeric time devices. The first couplet reflects Homer's lines translated by Pope as

> What-time the judge forsakes the noisy bar
> To take repast, and stills the wordy war.

But the dining of Homer's judges merely stilled the windy arguments; Pope's transformation makes something hideous and savage of their eighteenth-century heirs, who sacrifice lives under selfish compulsion of their own bodily hunger. Homer's words, that is, provide a standard of simple dignity against which Pope ironically measures the degeneracy of his own civilization. His second couplet is built on the lines he translated as

As the tir'd ploughman spent with stubborn toil,
Whose oxen long have torn the furrow'd soil,
Sees with delight the sun's declining ray,
When home with feeble knees, he bends his way
To late repast, (the day's hard labour done). (*Odyssey*, XIII, 39–43)

One need only recall Pope's opposition of agrarian cultural values to those of modern City capitalism in the *Epistle to Bathurst* to recognize the significance of his displacing Homer's ploughman by the merchant at the Royal Exchange. In the effete London culture the day's hard manual labor of Homer's ploughman is not performed by the merchant but by the lady at her dressing-table. Pope's lines of course are explicit enough and carry their own satiric force, but we lose the large historico-cultural context in which Pope has placed them unless we can see how they do violence to Homer's passages, adulterate them, because the weak and sordid modern culture adulterates the simple purity of the Homeric life. In fact, then, the text cannot properly be separated from its allusion, and the latter is present as a functional part of the sense.

The shearing of Belinda's lock, that trivial thing giving rise to the poem's mighty contest, is sufficiently colored by Pope, even in the poem's title, to take on ambiguous sexual nuances and to grant Belinda some seeming justification for her tantrums. It would not be irrelevant or unilluminating at this point to invoke Krafft-Ebing on the role of hair in primitive fertility and puberty rites, but we might more pertinently ask what the loss of maiden locks would more consciously have suggested to an audience whose natural and instinctive reference was the Greco-Roman literature and culture. Readers of Apollonius' *Argonautica* (IV, 26 seq.) would have known that when Medea planned to elope with Jason she tore off a long tress of hair and left it in her bedchamber for her mother, a memorial, the poet says, of her maidenhood. The annotators would have reminded the reader that Euripides, Herodotus, Callimachus, Valerius Flaccus, Pausanias, and Lucian, among others, also tell of nations whose maidens cut their virgin locks and sacrificed them to a deity of chastity as a ritualistic preparation for marriage. In the words of Statius, "by ancestral rite the daughters of Iasus, so soon as their chaste years grew ripe for wedlock, were wont to make offering of virgin tresses, and pray pardon for their first marriage-bed." [1] Because the hair had been dedicated in childhood to a deity, it was regularly called *crinis sacer*— the "sacred lock," as Belinda's is twice called (III, 153; IV, 133). These were facts known to any serious reader: the major edition of Statius,

[1] *Thebaid*, II, 253 seq.

by Casper Barth, contains an essay on the subject, and encyclopedias like Theodor Zwinger's *Theatrum humanae vitae* and Johann Hofmann's *Lexicon universale* treated it at some length.

In such a context of nuptial rites, what the Baron has raped is not Belinda's virginity but, like her fillet (IV, 101), the ritualistic sign of it. Since one normally subsumes the other, Pope can equivocate by innuendo, and John Dennis was on the right track without knowing it when he complained that the poet should have asked what strange motive could *induce* or *provoke* "A well-bred *Lord* t'assault a gentle *Belle*" (I, 8). "The Word *compel*," Dennis astutely observed, "supposes the Baron to be a Beast, and not a free agent." But from Belinda's point of view, although she has not lost her virginity in fact, she has lost what in her values transcends it, the totemic lock whereby society presumes her an unmarried maiden and grants her the corresponding rights and privileges. For her world is made up of the beau monde's conventional signs, decorative and playful, that substitute for flesh-and-blood reality—one in which a rouged cheek surpasses a real blush, sword-knots duel instead of swords, wigs content instead of beaux, a card game takes the place of the contest of the sexes, China jars stand for virginity, and a mirror reflection transcends the viewer. Hence, because Belinda equates "honor" not with the facts but with society's presumptions formed on the basis of these signs, she would rather have sacrificed "Hairs less in sight" than those which totemically endow her with maidenhood's power to domineer heartlessly over men, a power she is determined to retain.

To preserve that dominance, Belinda is fortified with the means of sublimating any heterosexual impulse. The resolute coquette, according to the Rosicrucian theology, is rewarded for her virginity with the (purely imaginary) sexual embraces of ambivalent sylphs, the disembodied souls of deceased coquettes. In addition, Belinda is provided with a chaste surrogate for a husband in Shock, the lap-dog equated by the poem with lover and husband (I, 15–16; III, 158). Notably a mass of hair, the breed derives its generic name from the Icelandic word whose sense we retain in "a shock of hair" and thus is related to the sexual symbolism of the lock. This theriomorphic husband-substitute, appropriately located in the lap, is Belinda's fetish, for, as the system of incubus-like sylphs makes clear, she is wedded to and sexually gratified by her own virginity; and the fact answers John Dennis' objection that a lesser sylph is assigned to guard the favorite lock while Ariel himself attends this "vile *Iseland Cur*."

The motive for the narcissistic coquette's desire to remain seemingly inviolate and therefore independent is obviously her pride, and its quasi-theological quality is defined by Ariel's whispering into her ear

a dream of her importance in the same way that Milton's Satan tempts
Eve in a dream:

> fair Angelic *Eve,*
> . . . be henceforth among the Gods
> Thyself a Goddess, not to Earth confin'd. (*P.L.,* V, 74–78)

But Ariel—that is, the coquettish humor in Belinda's femininity—also
tempts her with words that arouse other allusive reverberations defining her pride more precisely. According to the standard interpretation of the Gospel, the "babes" to whom divine mysteries are revealed
through faith are the humble and modest untainted by carnal wisdom,
and the "wise and prudent" from whom it is hid are those with a
swelling conceit of their worldly knowledge. This Scriptural metaphor
for humble faith Ariel perverts into its literal sense, childish ignorance
of human nature:

> Some secret Truths from Learned Pride conceal'd,
> To Maids alone and Children are reveal'd. (I, 37–38)

Then through this ignorant credulity, instead of faith ("The Fair
and Innocent shall still believe"), he reveals to Belinda the mysteries
of a religion of unrealistic and antisocial chastity. But the basic tenet
of this religion of the naïve is not Christian humility but pride: "thy
own Importance know, / Nor bound thy narrow Views to Things
below" (I, 35–36).

Now, "thy own Importance know" pointedly inverts the ubiquitous
doctrine that it is essential to "Know Thyself," which was consistently
interpreted as the true act of humility and regularly opposed to the
pride of curiosity, especially about the stars—the things *above.* The
common exemplar of pride in suprahuman learning as opposed to
humble self-knowledge was the astronomer Thales, who, gazing on the
stars above, nearly fell into a ditch. And of course the opposition ac-
counts for Raphael's refusal to explain to Milton's Adam the motions
of the stars:

> joy thou
> In what he [God] gives to thee, this Paradise
> And thy fair Eve: Heaven is for thee too high
> To know what passes there; be lowly wise:
> Think only what concerns thee and thy being (*P.L.,* VIII, 170–75)

—advice that leads Adam to tell of his own creation, loneliness for
society, and union with Eve, whereas Ariel advocates antisocial self-
sufficiency: know how important you are and disregard the human
world below, together with its sexual and marital needs. The per-

sistence of this moral antinomy and its relevance to Pope's social theme can be judged by Johnson's *Rambler* No. 24 (9 June 1750), which contrasts the "vanity or curiosity" of "calculating the weight of the terraqueous globe" and "adjusting successive systems of worlds beyond the reach of the telescope" with the self-knowledge leading to the performance of "those offices by which the concatenation of society is preserved, and mutual tenderness excited and maintained."

Moreover, if Ariel's advice to know one's own importance is a Satanic inversion of humble self-knowledge, so, conversely, is his instruction *not* to bind "thy narrow View to Things below." As Plutarch wrote in one of the major *loci* of the doctrine, to "know thyself" means to "use one's self for that one thing for which Nature has fitted one";[2] and exactly what Belinda is most fitted for and what is radical for Pope in the carnal world that Belinda ought to accept is intimated by "Things below," a term we may let Swift explicate for us. Spiritual ascent (like that advocated by Ariel), Swift wrote, "is not the Business of Flesh and Blood; it must by the necessary Course of Things, in a little Time, let go its hold, and fall into Matter. Lovers, for the sake of Celestial Converse . . . pretend to see Stars and Heaven in Ladies Eyes, and to look or think no lower." Such lovers "seem a perfect Moral to the Story of that Philosopher [that is, Thales], who, while his Thoughts and Eyes were fixed upon the Constellations, found himself seduced by his *lower Parts* into a *Ditch.*" No one who had read at least his Juvenal—to say nothing of the *Priapeia*—would have failed to understand the real meaning of *fossa,* or ditch, any more than he would have failed to understand Pope's "Things below."

Awakening from her dream vision of Ariel, Belinda immediately proceeds to the "sacred Rites of Pride" at the dressing-table. As the fact that the toilet is "unveil'd" indicates, we are here at the temple's inner shrine, where the idol of the goddess is kept, and the silver vases of cosmetics correspond to the sacred vases on the pagan altars. The mirror in which Belinda sees herself as a goddess is, of course, the traditional emblem of Pride, but, given the whole context of the mystery rites, it is probable that the scene Pope has painted can be identified more precisely. Apuleius described a procession of Isis in which some women with mirrors on their backs walked ahead of the priestesses and the idol of the goddess so that the goddess could see the priestesses as though they were advancing toward her. Other priestesses, he adds, made gestures as though combing and adorning the goddess' hair. Seneca ridiculed the women in the temple of Juno who hold up a mirror to the goddess; and Augustine, quoting a lost work by Seneca on superstition, similarly mocked the women who hold up mirrors to Juno and Minerva and in pantomime dress the hair of the goddesses. Not unexpectedly, the editors made cross references to these three *loci* of the theme, while one encyclopedia quoted Apuleius' description under the heading of "Speculum" as an example of "Vanitatem Foventia," and another, referring to all three passages, defined "Speculum Junoni tenere" as "vanitas." Supplied with a topos for the rites of pride, Pope solved the mystery of the immaterial goddess by identifying the attendant priestess who holds the mirror with the goddess who appears in it, and the ridiculed rite has become one of self-adoration.

However exquisite the sylphan machinery, it must also be recognized as demonic, and in tempting Belinda to transcend the flesh-and-blood world by lifelong chastity Ariel offers her a Satanic substitute for Christianity, complete with doctrine of immortality, angelology, psalmody, and cosmology. For example, he promises that if she is faithful to his doctrines of coquetry the sylphs will keep her

> Safe from the treach'rous Friend, the daring Spark,
> The Glance by Day, the Whisper in the Dark; (I, 73–74)

and his words invoke Psalm 91, promising that God "shall give his angels charge over thee" so that "Thou shalt not be afraid for the terror by night; nor for the arrow that flieth by day; Nor for the pestilence that walketh in darkness; nor for the destruction that wasteth at noonday"—threats regularly interpreted as covert and overt temptations. And just as the same Psalm promises the faithful that guardian angels will "keep thee in all thy ways," Ariel translates the coquette's social whirl into the wandering motions of the planets and the guardian sylphs into those angelic Intelligences who are supposed to guide the spheres:

> Oft when the World imagine Women [like the planets] stray,
> The Sylphs thro' mystic Mazes guide their Way,
> Thro' all the giddy Circle they pursue,
> And old Impertinence expel by new. (I, 91–94)

What the metaphoric activity of the poem is constituting is, of course, the prideful image of Belinda as an independent world and female society as a self-sufficient scheme. Belinda is imaged as the ruling sun, a deity who creates order by fiat ("Let Spades be Trumps! she said, and Trumps they were," III, 46), a mortal priestess who is her own divinity. As goddess of Pride she receives offerings from the entire world because she is its supreme deity. To the world she governs, the cup and coffee are "*China's* Earth" and its "smoking Tyde" (III, 110); for her "all *Arabia* breathes from yonder Box" (I, 134); and the Hindu emblem of the world, the elephant mounted on the tortoise, becomes her ivory and tortoise-shell comb. Female society is an entire planetary system, or a cosmos governed by the divine "*Cosmetic* Pow'rs"; and just as Belinda is her own goddess and is urged by Ariel to be sexually self-sufficient, the souls of coquettes are supposed to become the guardian angels of coquettes in a self-perpetuating scheme of female chastity and immortality.

The religion of such an exclusively coquette world obviously depends upon the rejection of all men, for in this theology they, not woman, are the cause of the Fall: "oh Pious Maid beware! . . . Beware of all, but most beware of Man" (I, 112–14)—which also nicely misapplies Christ's advice to the Apostles: "But beware of men: for they will deliver you up to the councils, and they will scourge you in their synagogues" (Matt. 10: 16–17). The resolute coquette both aspires to an exclusively female society like that of the Amazons and inverts hierarchy by usurping man's place. Consequently when Belinda seeks to overcome two adventurous knights she resorts to Ombre, a game deriving its name from the fact that the challenger, who also determines the governing trumps, is called *ombre*—the man. The reason, according to the standard handbook of that day, is that the game requires "Thought and Reflection which are Qualities peculiar to Man." Endowed with a lock which is itself the "Destruction of Mankind" (II, 19), Belinda has arrogated to herself man's role and in the sex-game of Ombre plays her cards to vanquish him at his own game. Not only is she aided in the battle against the beaux by Thalestris, queen of the Amazons—the "fierce Virago" (V, 37), or manlike woman—but in burning "At *Ombre* singly" to defeat the knights (III, 27) she identifies herself with Virgil's Amazon, Camilla, who volunteered "singly" to engage the opposing cavalry. Indeed, when Pope writes that the Baron prayed "Soon to obtain, and long possess" the lock and that

> The Pow'rs gave Ear, and granted half his Pray'r,
> The rest, the Winds dispers'd in empty Air, (II, 44–46)

he exactly repeats Virgil's words when Arruns prays to slay that same belligerent Camilla, notable for her love of virginity and weapons of war.[3] The Amazon is the perfect type of the coquette, implying the fantasy of a self-sufficient female society, ever victorious over men in the sex-battle.

[3] *Aeneid*, XI, 792–95, 583.

Marriage would of course shatter this proud fantasy by subjugating the coquette to man and destroying her power over fashionable society; and the theme of marriage, explicit in Clarissa's speech, hovers suggestively over the poem in the allusive contexts. A notable instance is the Cave of Spleen episode, which draws into its ambience the section of Virgil's seventh book in which Juno calls up the Fury Alecto to anger Lavinia's mother, Amata. Now, Belinda had been equated with Juno at the very beginning of the poem when the poet asked, "And in soft Bosoms dwells such mighty Rage?" (I, 12), for the line echoes Virgil's "tantaene animis caelestibus irae?" (*Aeneid*, I, 11), which questions how Juno, a divinity, can entertain the human passion of hate. Consequently Pope's adaptation not only expresses wonder that anger can lodge in Belinda's feminine tenderness but also carries an allusive oversense intimating Belinda's supreme divinity and attaching to her Juno's unforgiving resentment of Aeneas and his entire race. In *Aeneid*, VII, the source of the Cave of Spleen episode, Umbriel-like Alecto, on being called up by Juno, inspires Lavinia's mother and her female friends to Bacchic fury like that of Belinda and her attendant belles and incites the war that occupies the last half of the *Aeneid* as it does the end of the *Rape*. What is centrally significant in the context of the allusion is that Juno stirred up these angry battles because, in her enmity to Aeneas, she wished to thwart by that means his fated marriage with Lavinia.

Given Belinda's Amazonian character, the totemism of her "sacred" prenuptial lock, and the fact that the Cave of Spleen episode alludes to a context having to do with preventing a marriage, it is implicit that Belinda is not fighting off sexual union so much as the humiliation of marriage and its degrading social consequences. As a coquette, Belinda "rejects Mankind" (I, 68), seeking only "to win hearts and throw 'em away, regarding nothing but the triumph," and her antithesis is Clarissa, who, adapting Sarpedon's rationale for the heroic life, urges that she use "good Sense" and "good Humour" to preserve the men's admiration and desire that "Beauty gains," whatever maiden locks or maidenhood may be lost in the process. The advice is open to jaundiced interpretation, and the coquette's ally, Amazonian Thalestris, chooses to take it as that of a prude, who, by the poem's definition, seeks suitors only to jilt them successively in an insatiable hope for an ever more splendid husband. But in fact Clarissa's speech does "open more clearly the Moral of the Poem" by calling on Belinda to recognize that the coquette's mastery over men cannot outlast her transient beauty and that if she were to accept with heroic good humor the rape of the prenuptial lock as the inevitable risk of being a seductive and most nubile belle she would preserve, not lose, her glorious

power over men. Moreover, Clarissa openly acknowledges the value of
undertaking a "Huswife's Cares" as the heroic sacrifice that makes
female life meaningful and glorious in a world where beauty cannot
last. Belinda's life of privileged artifice cannot forever evade reality;
indeed, it tempts it, challenges it to break in. Therefore only when
Belinda rejects Clarissa's advice out of hand does the conflict of belles
and beaux develop into a real and physical sexual battle—the *nocturnum bellum,* as Virgil styles it—in which a finger and a thumb
can provoke an orgasmic sneeze that subdues the hero's "manly
Strength" and the hero, who had sought only "on his Foe to die,"
admits to the heroine,

> Nor think, to die dejects my lofty Mind;
> All that I dread, is leaving you behind!
> Rather than so, ah let me still survive,
> And burn in Cupid's Flames,—but burn alive. (V, 99–101)

Whether or not the coquette submits to marriage, her pretty fantasy
of self-sufficient virginity will inevitably be invaded by fleshly ap-
petites—to give evidence of Clarissa's truism that "she who scorns a
Man, must die a Maid." On this occasion, it is true, the heroine has
foiled the bodily assault with an epic trick, but the true wretchedness
of her state is made apparent by her cry:

> *Restore the Lock!* she cries; and all around
> *Restore the Lock!* the vaulted Roofs rebound. (V. 103–104)

Despite her victory over the Baron, Belinda, by scorning Clarissa's
advice, has reduced herself to the pitiable condition of Ovid's young
girls who fancy they are being earnestly wooed, only to find that their
elegant suitors are inflamed only by desire to steal their robes:

> *Redde meum!* clamant spoliatae saepe puellae,
> *Redde meum!* toto voce boante foro.

Another allusion exercises a structural control like that of the
Alecto episode. When, at Ombre, the virgin fends off the temptation
diamonds hold out to female hearts, halts at the brink of losing her
heart, and then defeats the men, she exults with pride; and the poet,
playing on "Honours" as both trophies of war and card honors, warns:

> Oh thoughtless Mortals! ever blind to Fate,
> Too soon dejected, and too soon elate!
> Sudden these Honours shall be snatch'd away,
> And curs'd for ever this Victorious Day. (III, 101–104)

As we know, this exactly echoes Virgil's prophecy when Turnus slays
Aeneas' companion Pallas and, exulting, seizes Pallas' belt as his
"honor," or trophy. Virgil's prophecy is fulfilled, for at the end of the
Aeneid when Aeneas hesitates in pity over the fallen Turnus it is the
sight of the stolen belt that incites him to slay his foe. Belinda
similarly pays for her proud honors, for the Baron later swears never
to return the severed hair:

> But by this Lock, this sacred Lock I swear,
>
> .   .   .   .   [*]   [*]   [*]
> Which never more its Honours shall renew,
>
> .   .   .   .   *]
> He spoke, and speaking, in proud Triumph spread
> The long-contended Honours of her Head (IV, 133–40)

—the *honores capitis*, as the Ancients described splendid hair. The
honor Belinda won at Ombre is the coquette's societal reputation defined by Thalestris as greater than virtue and by Ariel as the woman-
created system of chastity. And it is lost as far as coquette society is
concerned when the sign of virginal independence—the *honor capitis*
—is removed. The multiple puns on "honor" link Belinda's card
victory with the rape to reveal that the causal sequence in the *Aeneid*
is implicit here: the coquette's tempting conduct whereby she "con-
quers" men and gains honors should, indeed, lead to her being con-
quered by a man and losing those honors, but in marriage, not in the
nocturnum bellum of the last canto. Belinda's flaw, as Clarissa makes
clear, is not her pretty and domineering coquetry, but her refusal to
accept as its proper consequence the Baron's compulsion to rape the
social insignia of her virginal independence.

But even if we recognize that Pope's applying Virgil's prophecy to
Belinda does more than provide the reader the delight of recognition
and is also a structural control relating her acquisition of honors to
the price she must pay for them, the question remains how much of
the allusive context may properly be brought to bear. If we can assume that it is the nature of Pope's poetry to incite the reader to
search the allusive context for even those relevances not verbally engaged in his text, then it is strikingly apposite that Virgil's analogue
to the fateful honors Belinda won at Ombre—that is, the belt that
Turnus took from his slain foe and that was eventually responsible
for his own death—had depicted on it the story of Danaus' heroically
coquettish daughters who were forced into marriage by Aegyptus' sons
and slew their husbands on their bridal night (*Aeneid*, X, 495–99).
A number of the allusive contexts, however, prove curiously at odds

with the poem's explicit words. When, for example, the lock has been stolen, the poet writes,

> But anxious Care the pensive Nymph opprest,
> And secret Passions labour'd in her Breast.

These words, opening the fourth Canto, exactly repeat those opening the fourth *Aeneid*: "But the queen [i.e., Dido], long since wounded by anxious cares . . . is torn by secret passion." The parallel is exact, for Servius and the commentators who followed him, troubled by Virgil's beginning a book with "But," explained that Dido's anxious cares are being contrasted with Aeneas' easy indifference at the end of Book III, just as Belinda's cares contrast with the Baron's exultation over the rape at the end of Canto III. Moreover, just as Belinda is perturbed because the loss of her totemic lock undermines her social authority as coquette, so, according to Servius' gloss, Virgil here indicates Dido by her title (*regina*) rather than by name because the source of her cares threatens her dignity as queen. But Belinda grieves because a rejected beau has ravished her sign of maidenhood; Dido, who has vowed to remain faithful to her dead husband and never to remarry, grieves because she reluctantly finds she loves Aeneas. If the allusive context is truly operative, it suggests that beneath the outrage over the social offense and a determination to avoid love and marriage, Belinda, like Dido, feels a reluctant desire for the man, a passion hidden from her conscious mind. To what other feelings could Pope, repeating Virgil's very words, be referring as "secret Passions"? Surely not Belinda's resentment over the rape, which her shrieks have declared publicly enough. The same relation between Dido's failure to keep her lover and Belinda's failure to keep her sign of coquettish heartlessness is, of course, again developed when Belinda's lament is made to echo Dido's "Happy! ah too happy had I been if the Dardan keels had never touched these shores!" (*Aeneid*, IV, 657–58):

> Happy! ah ten times happy, had I been,
> If Hampton-Court these Eyes had never seen! (V, 149–50)

It is likely therefore that when Belinda, almost immediately after this cry, wishes,

> Oh had I rather un-admir'd remain'd
> In some lone Isle, or distant *Northern* Land, (IV, 153–54)

we are meant to hear Dido sigh, "Ah, that I could not live a blameless life outside wedlock, even as some wild beast, knowing not such cares!" (*Aeneid*, IV, 550–51). If so, the oversense vividly comments on the

unnatural and antisocial character of Belinda's wishes to avoid wedlock.

Later Belinda's grief over the rape is again set in the context of
Dido's love-griefs. Pathetically she demands the return of the lock, but
although "the pitying Audience melt in Tears, . . . *Fate* and *Jove*
had stopp'd the *Baron's* Ears" (V, 1–2). This echoes the failure of
Anna's pleas on Dido's behalf—"but by no tearful pleas is [Aeneas]
moved . . . Fate opposes, and Jove stops his ears" *(Aeneid*, IV, 438–
40)—and Pope makes the allusion explicit:

> Not half so fixt the Trojan cou'd remain,
> When Anna begg'd and Dido rag'd in vain.

But Belinda, rejecting the Baron, wants her maidenly honor returned;
Dido's raging desire is that her lover return. Pope's words and their
allusive context contradict each other, and if we take the contradiction
as the conflict between Belinda's conscious and subconscious mind, it
only confirms Pope's psychoanalysis of her elsewhere. When, for example, Ariel, guardian of virginal coquettes, seeks to prevent the
rape,

> Sudden he view'd, in spite of all her Art,
> An Earthly Lover lurking at her Heart. (III, 143–44)

Surely it is irrelevant to ask whether the lover is the Baron. Despite
the conscious social artfulness of her mind, Belinda is flesh and blood,
not a sylph, and in the Nature of her heart lurks unconscious yearning
for a mortal lover, not the imaginary, disembodied one Ariel offered.
In Ariel's religion there is sin in Belinda's Nature, and his powers over
her integrity fail. After all, Belinda never was Ariel's star pupil: in
spite of the dream in which he taught her to beware of all men, when
her "Eyes first open'd on a *Billet-doux* . . . all the Vision vanish'd
from [her] Head" (I, 118–20). As Pope paints her, she is at that age
when she thinks she hates the boys and cannot understand what is
really troubling her. "What mov'd my Mind," she asks in all innocence, "with youthful Lords to rome?" (IV, 159). . . .

Superficially, the elaborate comparison at the end of the poem (V,
129–40) of Belinda's lock to that of Catullus' Berenice seems only a
charming compliment: the severed lock, like Berenice's, becomes a
star; the astrologer Partridge, like Catullus' astronomer, discovers it;
and lovers hail it in the heavens. But in fact the comparison is highly
paradoxical, and the differences are even more functional than the
similarities. Belinda is outraged by the beau's seizure of her lock,
Berenice volunteered to sacrifice hers to the goddess of love for the
safe return of her husband; and Belinda is related to Berenice in the

same way that she is to Dido. Even within Pope's text it is incongruous that the "blest Lover" should mistake for Venus, goddess of love, the stellar lock of the coquette who had rejected a lord; and the line must be read tongue-in-cheek.

Moreover, Berenice's lock calls on wives who reverence their chaste wedlock to make offerings to it, adding, "But I want no offerings from those given to foul adultery"; Pope, on the other hand, pretending flattery, calls on the "blest Lover" to send up vows to Belinda's lock from "*Rosamonda*'s Lake"—a curious choice in view of the Fair Rosamond's adulterous affair with Henry. For under the guise of flattering Belinda, Pope is subtly giving body to Clarissa's axiom that "she who scorns a Man, must die a Maid," and the conclusion of the poem is far less the glitering tribute to Belinda than its beguiling surface claims. But now, as a working hypothesis, let us assume that by invoking Catullus' poem Pope implicitly invokes all of it that may be relevant. Just as Belinda's rejection of a possible lover is cast in terms of Dido's yearning for her lover, so, in one of the most striking passages of Catullus' poem, Berenice's lock asks, "Do new brides really hate Venus? or do they mock their parents' joys with hypocritical tears when they leave their virgin chambers? By the gods, they do not really grieve. This is what Berenice taught me by her real tears when her husband left her bed for the wars." Montaigne, incidentally, quoted these lines to illustrate the paradox "That we weep and laugh for the same thing." The bride's lamentation is veiled jubilation.

Indeed, Pope's enigmatic epigraph has all along been intimating the disparity between Belinda's conscious rejection of mankind and the unconscious stirrings of desire for a man. Pope substituted Belinda for one Polytimus in an epigram by Martial so that it translates: "I was reluctant, Belinda, to cut off your lock; but I am happy to have granted this to your wishes." Perhaps Mistress Arabella Fermor was to be beguiled into taking this as a charming tribute: the poet regrets that, poetically speaking, he has cut off her lock, but he is happy to have written the poem as she requested. But it is not what the lines actually say: Polytimus begged Martial to cut off his hair, and Martial did so, adding in the two lines Pope omitted that now his real beauty has been made visible, just as Pelops, by being shorn, bared his beautiful shoulder to his new bride. Now, the standard commentary on Martial in at least twenty editions up to and including the handsome variorum of 1617 was that of Calderinus, who explains that Polytimus asked the poet to cut his lock because he intended to get married. In view of the general tenor of the other allusive contexts, the relevance of Calderinus' interpretation to Belinda seems fairly obvious.

If this has been an admissible commentary on *The Rape of the*

Lock, it would imply that the mode of existence of Pope's poetry—and probably of many other neoclassic poems—ought to be defined broadly enough to include a creative act by the reader. For it suggests that the reader is not only to appreciate the poet's invention in finding appropriate allusions but is actively invited by them to exercise, within poetic reason, his own invention by contemplating the relevances of the entire allusive context and its received interpretation. Instead of making the passive assumption, for example, that Pope omitted the last two lines of Martial's epigram because they are not applicable, one is to entertain the possibility that their omission is an enticement to the reader to exercise as much wit as the poet did in applying the first two lines to his poem. Certainly when Pope, like some others, printed the Latin originals along with his imitations of Horace, he was prodding the reader to discover for himself the ways in which the Latin text implicitly acts upon the English, synergistically qualifying, incrementing, and complicating its sense and tone. Sterne was not the first to ask the reader to "give me all the help you can" and to "halve this matter amicably" so that both author and reader have "something to imagine." One might instance the function of the tunes in Gay's *Beggar's Opera* in drawing their original lyrics into significant interaction with Gay's words; or, to select an especially complex example, the consequences of placing Pope's line "And one more Pensioner St. Stephen gains" (*Epistle to Bathurst,* l. 394) in the *total* context both of the Scriptural story of St. Stephen and of Juvenal's Third Satire, which it echoes. One might also consider the fact that when Gulliver wishes to testify to the truthfulness of his book and to avow that he has followed the virtuous example of the rational horses, he quotes the lines from the *Aeneid* in which Sinon protests that he is incapable of deceit. Surely the reader is expected to recall that Sinon was, in fact, the most heroic of liars and that through his deceitful protestation of truthfulness he persuaded the Trojans to admit another kind of fictitious horse—to the destruction of their city. Such literature as this is constituted not only by its own verbal texture but also by the rich interplay between the author's text and the full contexts it allusively arouses, for these allusive resonances are not peripheral but functional to the meaning of the artistic product.

Mythopoeic Activity in the *Rape of the Lock*

by *Rebecca P. Parkin*

In the *Rape of the Lock* divinity is in varying degrees postulated of almost everything—of Belinda, the Baron, the Scissors, the sparkling Cross, the Lap-Dog, the Petticoat, and the Lock, as well as of Love, Fate, Jove, and the Sylphs and Gnomes with all pertaining to them. The finite realm of beaux and belles and the most trivial objects in their surroundings are presented as larger than mortal, shot through, so to speak, with the Infinite. Even Belinda's patch-box, which falls thrice from her hand as a warning, is a thing "possessed." Like the tottering china that shakes without a wind, it functions on a superhuman as well as a human level. And the Sylphs and Gnomes, creatures of fantasy though they are, are as real as feminine beauty, frailty, and "honor" or as frustration, malice, and mischief in the human heart.

The ground of reader assent to this seemingly contradictory presentation is in part Pope's use of the classical epic framework. In the Homeric world everything that exists, whether stationary or kinetic in its mode of being, is sacredly alive. Everything is Zeus-linked—"they in Zeus and He in them." All the phenomena of nature, even bread, grass, and the dawn, are holy.

To this Pope adds, especially by his frequent Miltonic echoes, the world of Christian miracle—the world in which angels may appear bodily to instruct man and the devil converse in the form of a toad; a world in which the eating of an apple can entail consequences enormously disproportionate if considered without reference to the special qualities of that apple.

Together, the Homeric and Christian myths help suggest a spiritual approach to reality and particularly to human affairs, preparing the way for mythopoeic action. The solemn theological postulate that the divine is concerned with man and the things of man because in some way the divine is *in* man is, of course, treated in terms of puffs, powders, patches, and billets-doux. In an age skittish about a direct approach to the world of usual life as a divine mystery this is a telling way to deal with such matters. Pope furthers this indirect, seemingly not too serious approach by keeping Christian mythology subordinate to the Graeco-Roman and Rosicrucian systems.

Divinity is most prominently embodied in the person of Belinda. Intimations of her divinity range from such conventionalized "sleeping" etymological expressions as the hope that she, like the goddess Muse, will "inspire" Pope's lays, to the celebrated scene of the sacred rites of her toilet.

The establishment of her divinity falls into three major classifications: the general deification of the sex to which she belongs; the special treatment accorded Belinda, such as the head Sylph's attendance, together with the superhuman value placed on everything connected with her, especially her "sacred Lock"; and finally, the insistence throughout the poem that she is a kind of sun goddess.

In Canto I we are told:

> Oft, when the world imagine women stray,
> The Sylphs through mystic mazes guide their way.

In addition to this divine guidance, women are said, when their role on earth is over, to return to their "first Elements." Termagants will become Salamanders, "soft yielding minds" Nymphs, prudes turn into Gnomes, and coquettes become airy Sylphs. During life the sex as a whole has Sylphic assistance:

> . . . to curl their waving hairs,
> Assist their blushes, and inspire their airs.

The gift of a lady to her knight, specifically Clarissa's offering of the scissors, is received "with rev'rence." When the Fair pay visits on "solemn" days "num'rous wax-lights in bright order blaze." Women are "Angels called, and Angel-like adored," and at the theater the side-box bows to them "from its inmost rows." When the belles engage in battle, they exhibit more than mortal powers—the power, indeed, of life and death. Enraged Thalestris "scatters death around from both her eyes." Chloe kills Sir Plume with a frown and then revives him with a smile.

But Belinda outshines all her sex in divine attributes and importance. She is told that she is the "distinguished care/Of thousand bright Inhabitants of Air." The head Sylph, Ariel himself, comes to warn her of the impending disaster. Her own "heav'nly image in the glass" is the goddess she worships during the sacred ceremony of her toilet. When the Baron desires a favor from her, he builds an altar to Love—which is, in a sense, Belinda herself.

Sylphs who are careless in attending Belinda are threatened with hellish punishments—all of them within Belinda's Rhadamanthine power: being "stopped in vials," "transfixed with pins," "plunged in lakes of bitter washes," and shrunk with alum styptics. When she is very angry lightning flashes from her eyes, and by the use of "Cosmetic Powers" she can make these lightnings keener.

Not only is her Lock sacred, but as the symbol of her chastity it is called an "inestimable prize." When it is lost, she "burns with more than mortal ire." Canto IV opens with a long list of grievances, many of them greater than the snipping of a curl; yet Belinda's rage at the loss of her Lock is said to exceed that of the victims of all these other grievances. This heightens the significance of her loss and exhibits her emotion about it as above the average mortal run for a mere ringlet. Finally, the surest "proof" the poem gives that the Lock is too exalted a trophy for a mere mortal is its ascension into heaven and its perpetual glorification there. Future lovers will send up vows to it and the fates of nations be foretold by its celestial motions.

Furthermore, Belinda and the objects associated with her can work miracles. Sailing forth on the Thames:

> On her white breast a sparkling Cross she wore,
> Which Jews might kiss, and infidels adore.

The kissing and adoration are in a sense miracles of the Cross—though of the sparkling not the bloody one. And this conversion of Jews and infidels is owing not to the power of Christ but to the force of female beauty. And somewhat like a deity willing to undergo tortures and to sacrifice himself for the good of mankind, Belinda points out that she bound her locks in "paper durance," wreathed her tender head with "torturing irons" and fillets, "And bravely bore the double loads of lead." The Baron himself petitions her for a miracle he is confident she can work. Rather than die, he begs:

> . . . ah let me still survive,
> And burn in Cupid's flames—but burn alive.

This brings us to the question of Belinda's Olympian pedigree, which it is possible to conjecture with some certitude. Repeatedly the poem suggests her kinship with the sun. In Canto I it is said that when she opens her eyes they will eclipse the sun. At the opening of Canto II this sun comparison is extended:

Not with more glories, in th'etherial plain,
The Sun first rises o'er the purpled main
Than, issuing forth, the rival of his beams
Launched on the bosom of the silver Thames.
Fair Nymphs, and well-drest Youths around her shone,
But every eye was fixed on her alone.

           *   *   *

Favours to none, to all she smiles extends;
Oft she rejects but never once offends.
Bright as the sun, her eyes the gazers strike,
And, like the sun, they shine on all alike.

Not only is she the center of this youthful solar system boating on the Thames; she has an effect like sunshine on the world as a whole: "Belinda smiled, and all the world was gay." However, not all her sun functions are benevolent. In Greek myth the daughters of the sun—such as Circe, Medea, and the nymphs who guard the cattle of Helios—are endowed with special terror. Like the sun itself, they possess a strong destructive power.

In Belinda the spell-binding and enchantment activities of a Circe and the thirst for cruel vengeance of a Medea are exerted, properly, only in the hyperbole of courtship. Her "cruelty" is directed, as a belle's must be, toward her beaux. She nourishes her shining locks for the "destruction of mankind"; and as the sun destroys with its rays, so Belinda can make fops "die" by glances from her eyes:

For after all the murders of your eye,
When, after millions slain, yourself shall die:
When those fair suns shall set, as set they must. . . .

These lines are particularly interesting since they also undercut the myth of Belinda's divinity—specifically her sunship—by references to her actual mortality. The time of the poem is conceived as a single day, its progress marked by frequent references to the progress of the sun in the sky. The implication is that Belinda's course, like the sun's, will ultimately end in darkness.

Pope frequently undercuts the beautiful or heroic structures he builds up, either in the interest of realism or to achieve shock or risibility. Here by the juxtaposition of two seemingly contradictory aspects of Belinda's nature, her divinity and her mortality, he makes this sun myth come to grips in a reverberating way with actuality.

For there is an actual level on which Belinda the woman, with all her frivolities, is divine. As a woman, she is a volitional, morally responsible part of God's universe. The good sense or lack of it which she brings to bear upon the great business of the Hampton Court scene—her selection of a husband—will have its effect upon her own future, that of her children, and ultimately of the human race. She is also the physical vehicle of that future. As such she is sacred in the same way as—but in an intenser degree than—Homer's "holy" grass, bread, and dawn.

It is necessary for Pope to begin by stressing Belinda's divinity. The affront offered her, slight in appearance, must be felt as a serious and real affront, as, in fact, sacrilege. The clipping of the lock must signify simultaneously not only a minor youthful folly but also, symbolically, the rape of a woman and the outrage of a goddess.

If Belinda's mortality were not also stressed, the myth of her sun-ship would lose much of its acceptability. Western civilization has tended to turn away from the conviction that everything that lives is God-related. The more enlightened of the Chinese and Indian traditions have never lost sight of this, and our own major poets have had to turn their eyes toward a unifying spiritual center. But the poet of an age of common sense may find it good strategy, as Pope did with Belinda, to qualify goddess-ship by emphasizing finite, human qualities. The scene at Belinda's dressing-table where she is both the mortal high priestess and the goddess worshiped in the mirror is an especially felicitous example of this strategy.

The miraculous power exerted by Belinda's eyes and the cross on her bosom has already been indicated. So potent is her beauty—for it is through the actual force of female beauty that her divinity operates—that a single hair from the belle's head can do wonders:

> Love in these labyrinths his slaves detains,
> And mighty hearts are held in slender chains.
> With hairy springes we the birds betray,
> Slight lines of hair surprise the finny prey,
> Fair tresses man's imperial race ensnare,
> And beauty draws us with a single hair.

This is at once miraculous and literally true. Sporting with the tangles of Neaera's hair is well recognized as synecdoche for the actual sexual attraction of the female for the male.

Within the field of this God-given attraction all the trivia connected with Belinda achieve accessory deity. Her powder, her washes, her fur-belows, and her blushes are sanctified, receiving the care of heavenly spirits. Her chastity too, under the metaphoric disguises of "some frail China jar" and the portentous Petticoat, attains mythic stature. Yet the very frailty and transience of blushes and chastity bring forcibly to mind this goddess's humanity.

The status of Shock as an object belonging to Belinda has particular interest in this connection. Ariel ends his review of dangers threatening the heroine with the climatic line: "Or whether Heaven has doomed that Shock must fall." In the context of this speech Shock's fall has been made to seem more important than Belinda's forgetting her prayers, losing her heart, or staining her honor. This impression is reinforced by Ariel's decision to assign lesser points of danger to lesser Sylphs. Early in the poem the foppish lovers are compared to lap-dogs —a minor theriomorphic myth which gains in importance when it becomes clear that to belles lap-dogs are in a sense lover substitutes. Thus the concern of Belinda and her guardian Sylph for Shock is not eccentric but a recognition of the belle's major interest in life—her relations with eligible men.

This is typical of the way values are deliberately confused in the poem. What appears trivial—the exaggerated anxiety over Shock—is actually significant; and conversely. When Belinda says: "Let Spades be trumps! . . . and trumps they were" she only seems to be going through the routine procedure of a card game. "Really" she is a goddess creating and lighting a world. These two meanings are linked by the fact that Belinda, representing generic woman, is the physical means by which the "little worlds" of mankind are brought into being. Her beauty and the feminine graces, of which this poem makes so much, actually are a "light" of daily living and one of the ordering forces of the world.

Though the poem focuses primary attention on the deity of Belinda, her male compeers also come under the cognizance of Olympus. Belinda's status is multiple. She is a belle, an epic champion, and a sun goddess. But the fops' elevation seems at first to go no further than the heroic—and even that is precarious. In the context of Hampton Court it is easier to believe in the ladies' divinity than in the fops' heroism. For the women, in spite of their frivolity, are functioning in an environment proper to them; whereas the men are out of a specific manly context. Their attributed heroism is nowhere exhibited unless in the Baron's surreptitious severing of Belinda's lock—an act which on the goddess level is sacrilege, on the epic level a war trick, and in the polite world a piece of rudeness.

Both in the game of cards and in the crowning battle fought with fans, snuff, and killing frowns these "heroes" are overcome by the ladies. Even Jove decides for the latter:

> Now Jove suspends his golden scales in air,
> Weighs the Men's wits against the Lady's hair;
> The doubtful beam long nods from side to side;
> At length the wits mount up, the hairs subside.

The myth of the beaux' heroism seems to be a mock-myth—one not substantiated in the action of the poem. But it would be mistaken to suppose that this pseudo-myth is not functional. On the contrary, the irony of its relation to actuality, compared to that of the Belinda myth, reinforces the theme of false and confused values. In the eyes of belles, these fops *are* god-like heroes. The belles, like certain other deities, are purblind.

Based also on imperfect vision are two twin myths which pervade the poem: that seeming is being, and conversely; and that the little is big, and conversely. Set against these myths of confused vision is the reader's correct view of actuality, the view in which appearances are seen through, where big things are always and everywhere big, and little ones always and everywhere little.

But the relation of these two myths to actuality is not simple. Within the "actuality" of the fashionable sphere in which Belinda moves, seeming *is* to some extent being and has real effects. If Belinda is to marry reputably, she must seem—but not necessarily be— "first in virtue as in face." Her virtue may be put on for public consumption as are her clothes and her complexion. On the other hand, though the belle may in reality be virtuous, if she is made to seem questionable—as by a fop's displaying a curl of hair snipped from her person—then her actual virtue, as Thalestris points out to her, counts for nothing.

> Methinks already I your tears survey,
> Already hear the horrid things they say,
> Already see you a degraded toast
> And all your honour in a whisper lost!
> How shall I, then, your helpless fame defend?
> 'Twill then be infamy to seem your friend!

As far as the fashionable world is concerned, big things, such as the loss of virtue, may have no important consequences; whereas little things, the snipping of a curl, may be disastrous. These twin ideological myths have a two-way connection with actuality: the actuality of the moral absolute and the actuality of the world of Sir Plume and Thalestris.

This conflict of actualities is reflected in the Rosicrucian machinery. Among other things, the Sylphs represent the fashionable actuality, and the Gnomes with the Cave of Spleen the vengeance absolute actuality always takes when flouted. It is this contrast of actualities which gives the poem its deepest significance.

The effectiveness with which the contrast functions derives not so much from the abstract truth underlying it as from the extent to which

ˮSylphs and Gnomes are liberated from fairyland and made denizens simultaneously of London and the New Jerusalem. Similarly, their human charges are inhabitants of fashionable London, relatives of Zeus, and pilgrims to eternity. It is this coming together of fictional and real, their interaction, and their partial fusion that helps give the *Rape of the Lock* its exceptional degree of integrated ambivalence.

A prime factor in achieving this richness without sacrificing unity is the care Pope takes to anchor each of the poem's nonce-myths in a variety of established mythologies. He borrows impartially from Greeks, Romans, Christians, Hebrews, and Rosicrucians—not to mention public or natural myth and such special areas as Shakespeare's world of diminutive fairies. Nor is it merely a question of mythological systems. The Cave of Spleen, for instance, has a rich overlay both of general underworld concepts and of visits to underworlds in specific poems. Yet all these diverse borrowings are subjugated to the particular purpose of Umbriel's visit to this particular Hades. It is the *curiosa felicitas* of Pope's design that the whirlwind of mythopoeic activity going on in the poem is so tempered by its presentation that on the surface it makes little more noise than a beau's whisper in the ear of a belle. Pope's own mythopoeic method is, in effect, this:

> When Florio speaks, what virgin could withstand,
> If gentle Damon did not squeeze her hand?

PART TWO

View Points

William Empson

[E]ighteenth-century ambiguity was essentially easy and colloquial; it was concerned to exploit, as from a rational and sensible mental state, the normal resources of the spoken language. Its possible grace and slightness may be shown by a fine detail from the *Rape of the Lock.* When Belinda wins at cards

> The nymph, exulting, fills with shouts the sky;
> The walks, the woods, and long canals reply.
> Oh thoughtless mortals, ever blind to fate,
> Too soon dejected, and too soon elate,
> Sudden these honours shall be snatched away,
> And cursed for ever this victorious day.

Reply may be transitive or intransitive. It is the poet who makes these classical reflections, but, as far as the grammar is concerned, the speaker may as well be the environs of Hampton Court, accustomed as they are to the fall of favourites and the brevity of human glory.

Such a use of the verb may be insisted upon by prepositions or adverbs placed where the different meanings are wanted; this needs no illustration, and my example is intended chiefly to show in how small a compass these typical devices may be employed.

> Oh, if to dance all night, and dress all day,
> Charmed the small pox, or chased old age away,
> Who would not scorn what housewives cares produce,
> Or who would learn one earthly thing of use?
>
> *(Essay on Women.)*

Here *charmed* at first means "fascinated," so as to make it sit still and do no harm, as one would do to snakes or one's husband; and then, because *chased* insists on the activity of this process, and because *away* is in a prominent position at the end of the line, *charmed* takes on a new meaning as *charmed away,* "removed entirely even when it had already arrived," no doubt by some apparently unreasonable incantation, as one does warts. It is these slight variations of suggestion, I think, that give vivacity to the line.

In the same way, the lyrical outburst of good sense that follows on from this plays continually on the border-line between the first and second types of ambiguity.

> But, since, alas, frail beauty must decay,

This insists it is reasonable by being a tautology: "in so far as beauty is frail it is exposed to decay"; but *frail* from its setting also carries a suggestion of moral as well as physical fragility, which continues to haunt the verses.

> Curled, or uncurled, since locks will turn to grey.

Locks may have been *curled* by art (or *uncurled* for that matter), or have been, to start with, (naturally) *curled;* so that we have now three ways of dividing up women—chaste-susceptible, from the first line; beautiful-ugly, if *uncurled* hair is out of fashion, and artificial-natural, from the second. *Will turn to grey* is in part a simple and inexorable future tense, the statement of Nature or the poet, and in part the metre makes it a statement of the lady; "It *will* turn to grey, the nasty stuff, I *can't* stop it."

> Since, painted, or not painted, all shall fade,

Artificial-natural, with its associate susceptible-chaste, is now strengthened against beautiful-ugly as the distinction in question, but not left in possession of the field; *painted* might be applied to "meads" in Pope's dialect, and had not quite lost the sense of "coloured from whatever cause."

The verb is now only future, as the place of the ambiguous *will* at the place of emphasis has been taken by *all.* Both these changes help the crescendo.

> And she who scorns a man must die a maid.

The wave as it breaks returns to tautology, from which the original beautiful-ugly criterion seems to have faded out. It may combine artificial-natural with wanton-chaste; "modesty and virtue are no security, because if you don't make the most of yourself you won't get a husband"; or may oppose them to one another; "artificiality and virtue are no security, because if you think yourself too fine for any of the available men you won't get a husband either." The tautology chiefly breaks down in its tenses, and thus implies that "you may not want a husband now, whether because you are too humble or too fanciful, too chaste or too gay, but in the end, every woman must admit it was what she needed." In this roundabout way, by not defining the relation between two criteria and leaving a loophole in a tautology, Pope arrives, as did Chaucer in flat sentences, at what may indeed be the fundamental commonplace of poetry, a statement of the limitations of the human situation. "Seeing then the inherent crudity of all possible earthly happiness, considering the humility of those demands which can alone hope to be satisfied . . ."

> What then remains, but well our power to use,
> And keep good humour still, whate'er we lose?

Well may mean "thoroughly" or "with moderation," and thus implies a sort of humility and *good humour* in deciding which of them is best in any particular situation. *Still* may mean that we must always keep our balance, always be prepared to laugh at the absurdity of the world and our own nature, or *keep* it *still* may mean that we must be careful not to laugh too publicly, to give ourselves away by not insisting on our dignity or our rights. Reviewing, finally, the three sets of opposites, we may *lose* beauty, refinement, or virginity, the lover we had desired, the privacy we had built up, or the husband it would have been wise to obtain.

Lawrence Babb

In *The Rape of the Lock,* Alexander Pope represents Spleen as a sullen goddess who holds court in a misty underworld cavern filled with apparitions and subsidiary personifications. Much of the meaning and connotation which the Augustans saw in this passage necessarily escapes the modern reader. It is my purpose to restore to it some of the colour which has faded from it. The malady which Pope's contemporaries called *spleen* (*vapours, hypochondria,* and *hysteria* were other names which they applied to it) had had a long history in medical tradition. Its theoretical existence had been due, ultimately, to Galen and Hippocrates, the ancient Greek physicians whose authority had dominated mediæval and Renaissance medicine. In England it

"The Cave of Spleen" by Lawrence Babb. From Review of English Studies, *XII (1936), 165–67, 175–76. Copyright 1936 by Clarendon Press. Reprinted by permission of the author and the Clarendon Press, Oxford. The footnotes have been deleted for the purposes of this edition.*

had been a fashionable complaint for over a century when Pope wrote
The Rape of the Lock. Until rather late in the seventeenth century,
it had been called *melancholy.* The conception of spleen current in
Queen Anne's England may be greatly clarified by a study of treatises
on melancholy written in Tudor and early Stuart times. One discovers
in these works that *melancholy* was a concept of some complexity. The
term was used to denote multifarious ills of body and mind supposed
to be due to the humour *melancholy,* or *black bile.* This humour was
described as the grosser part of the blood or as the dregs of the blood.
The office of the spleen (that is, of the organ of that name) was to
absorb and evacuate as much of it as was superfluous to the physiological operations. If there were too much of it in any part of the body
or in the system as a whole, it would cause melancholic disorders. Besides the melancholy of the normal physical state, there was believed
to be an *unnatural melancholy,* a noxious black humour produced by
the corruption of healthy humours. To this were attributed widely
diverse ailments, all of them called melancholy. The mental symptoms
of melancholy, it was supposed, were due principally to black vapours
which rose from the melancholic humours. These vapours ascended to
the brain and saturated it. They also sullied and damaged the *animal
spirits,* clear and subtle fluids which were believed to flow in the
nerves and to serve as a medium of communication between the mind
and the organs of sense and motion. In either case, the result was the
same: all of the images passing through the mind were discoloured.

*   *   *

Eighteenth-century spleen is the direct descendant, in medical tradition, of hypochondriacal melancholy. *Hypochondria* is one of the
eighteenth-century names for the disease. One can see the appropriateness of the terms *spleen* and *vapours.* One can understand, also, why
vapours float through Pope's Cave of Spleen and why his personified
malady lies with "Pain at her side." Presumably Pope means the left
side. . . .

So long as reason rules the wayward imagination, a touch of hypochondria "cannot but produce an excellent Genius." Indeed, "many
Hysterick Women owe their good Sense, ready Wit, and lively Fancy"
to their affliction. Spleen, then, is fittingly called "Parent . . . of
female wit" in *The Rape of the Lock,* and it is evident that she may
provoke either "th' hysteric, or poetic fit."

*   *   *

Although Pope satirized the affectations and absurdities of his supposedly splenetic countrymen, neither he nor his public doubted the

reality of the disease. Their notions regarding it may have been based to some extent upon observed phenomena. But for the most part their conception of spleen was compounded of elements drawn from the group of ideas traditionally associated with melancholia and from contemporary medical theory. Which elements came from these two sources respectively cannot be clearly determined, for the doctor, like the layman, owed many of his beliefs to tradition. The components which went into the Cave of Spleen had had not only a long history in scientific thought but also something of a literary history.

William Frost

The rhetoric of *The Rape of the Lock* is not only based on the rhetoric of the classical epic, but is based on it in such a way that an attentive Augustan reader, even though he might be unskillful in Greek and Latin, would instantly recognize Pope's language as epical if he were fairly well read in the English literature of the age. For example, in Pope's day the most celebrated recent contribution to the epic in English had been Dryden's translation of the *Aeneid* (1697), a work which Pope takes pains to echo unmistakably at a number of points in *The Rape of the Lock*. In the sixth book of the English *Aeneid*—to glance at one passage—the hero, on a tour of the underworld, visits the Elysian Fields, where he meets the souls of the blessed disporting themselves; and, in the midst of a description of their games, the following couplet occurs:

> The love of Horses, which they had, alive,
> And care of Chariots, after Death survive. (VI, 889 f.)

Early in the first book of *The Rape of the Lock,* Ariel describes to Belinda in a dream the future immortal existence of woman:

> Think not, when Woman's transient Breath is fled,
> That all her Vanities at once are dead; . . .
> Her Joy in gilded Chariots, when alive,
> And Love of *Ombre,* after Death survive. (I, 51 ff.)

Belinda is to have her own mock-Elysian Fields; and, as Pope's editor points out, the "Chariots" have acquired an effective double meaning

"The Rape of the Lock *and Pope's Homer" by William Frost. From* Modern Language Quarterly, *1947, pp. 342–44. Reprinted by permission of the author and publisher. The footnotes have been deleted for the purposes of this edition.*

from the fact that London carriages of Pope's own time were often so called.

Similarly, in the opening to Canto IV of *The Rape of the Lock* Pope means his readers to recall the opening of a more famous fourth book. "But anxious Cares the pensive Nymph opprest," he writes; just as Dryden had written "But anxious cares already seiz'd the Queen" (IV, 1)—and Belinda becomes another queenly Dido.

Dryden's *Aeneid* was not, of course, the only work whose English style Pope found suggestive of epic manner. The author of Genesis may not be strictly an heroic poet, but his famous sentence "And God said, 'Let there be light,' and there was light" (1:3) had been commended by Longinus as the very zenith of sublimity in literature —a commendation Pope did not forget when he wrote *"Let Spades be Trumps!* she said, and Trumps they were" (III, 46). In like manner, the frivolous clutter of Belinda's dressing table—"Puffs, Powders, Patches, Bibles, Billet-doux" (I, 138)—has its dignified ancestor in the horrific confusion of Milton's Hell: "Rocks, Caves, Lakes, Fens, Bogs, Dens, and Shades of Death" (*Paradise Lost,* II, 621). Still other works and authors laid under contribution for Pope's heroic diction were: Virgil's *Georgics,* Cowley's *Davideis,* Dryden's *The Hind and the Panther,* Ovid in several translations, Dryden's Juvenal, Lucan, Statius, Shakespeare, Chaucer, Donne.

Perhaps the most extended and sustained piece of epic parody in the whole poem, however, is based on a translation from ancient epic made by Pope himself: I refer to the famous speech of Clarissa at the beginning of the fifth canto of the *Rape,* which amounts to a delicate burlesque of the equally famous speech of Sarpedon, the Trojan captain, in the twelfth book of the *Iliad.* Before the appearance of *The Rape of the Lock,* this speech of Sarpedon to Glaucus had already been made familiar to eighteenth-century readers in three translations or adaptations: that of Motteux, the translator of *Don Quixote,* in *The Muse's Mercury,* Volume I (1707); that of John Denham, the author of *Cooper's Hill,* in 1668 (republished, as Professor Tillotson notes, in *Miscellany Poems, The First Part,* third edition, 1702); and that of Pope, in Tonson's *Poetical Miscellanies: The Sixth Part* (1709).

In view of the use which I shall show Pope to have made of certain passages in his as yet unpublished *Iliad* and *Odyssey,* it is interesting to note that of these three versions of Sarpedon's speech at hand, in print and familiar to him, it was his own which he chose as a model for Clarissa's phrasing. The most important echoes are the following:

Sarpedon.
> Why on those Shores are we with Joy survey'd . . .
> Unless great Acts superior Merit prove . . . ?
>
> (XII, 377, 379)

Clarissa.
> How vain are all these Glories, all our Pains,
> Unless good Sense preserve what Beauty gains. . . .
>
> (V, 15–16)

Sarpedon.
> 'Tis ours, the Dignity They [the Gods] give, to grace;
> The first in Valour, as the first in Place. . . .
>
> (XII, 381–82)

Clarissa.
> That Men may say, when we the Front-box grace,
> Behold the first in Virtue, as in Face!
>
> (V, 17–18)

Sarpedon.
> But since, alas, ignoble Age must come,
> Disease, and Death's inexorable Doom. . . .
>
> (XII, 391–92)

Clarissa.
> But since, alas! frail Beauty must decay,
> Curl'd or uncurl'd, since Locks will turn to grey. . . .
>
> (V, 25–26)

The second echo, involving as it does a surprise rime-word, is particularly subtle. The ear that remembers Sarpedon's speech—and we may be sure that Pope's ear, at least, remembered it clearly enough —expects "Behold the first in Virtue, as in *Place*"; and "Place," of course, would be a perfectly fitting word for Clarissa to use, in view of the "Front-box" of the preceding line. It would be more than fitting, in fact, it would be admirably satiric; for when Sarpedon speaks of his "Place," he is referring to his position among the generals and noblemen of Troy, whereas Clarissa is talking about a good seat at the theatre. But how much better, in the context of Clarissa's whole speech, is "Face"! Not only does it create the shock of surprise and of an unfamiliar, imaginative expression (in ordinary speech we do not customarily refer to a preëminent beauty as "the first in Face"), but it also throws Clarissa's emphasis precisely where Pope wants it: on *physical* beauty, the melancholy characteristic of which is its transitoriness:

> Curl'd or uncurl'd, since Locks will turn to grey,
> Since painted, or not painted, all shall fade. . . .

To call such writing as this a parody is almost to belittle it. Sarpedon's speech is predominantly heroic, Clarissa's elegiac; reminiscences of heroism blend into the elegy, forming one strain of its melancholy music. This is particularly true of the third parallel cited above. . . . For the reader and critic of *The Rape of the Lock,* today or two centuries ago—any time since the publication of his Homer—the second alternative is literal truth: for the fact is that *The Rape of the Lock* is a better parody because Pope later created (and by "created" I mean wrote and printed) some of the effects he parodied in it.

William Kurtz Wimsatt, Jr.

Pope in Chapters X and XI of *Peri Bathous* wrote a comic treatment of "Tropes and Figures" (including "The Antithesis, or See-Saw"), and he once observed to Spence that the "stiffness of style" in Wycherley's plays was "occasioned by his always studying for antithesis." But neither in his *Essay on Criticism,* nor in his remarks to Spence, nor in his letters, even the elaborate letter on versification to Walsh, has Pope anything substantial to say about the system of artful figures which later critics have considered characteristic of his couplets. Pope talks of the metrical "niceties," of suiting the sound to the sense, of caesura, of expletives, and of hiatus, or of avoiding extravagance in diction. The rhetorical sinews of the kind of verse in which he was the champion—the essential patterns where Waller's strength and Denham's sweetness joined, where Dryden had achieved the long resounding march and energy divine—these perhaps had been learned so well by Pope as a boy that he could forget them. "It was our family priest," he told Spence, "who taught me the figures, accidence, and first part of grammar." In later life perhaps the figures were assumed by Pope under the general head of "correctness." At any rate he seems to have been able to take them for granted.

Among the hundred odd figures, "auricular," "sensable," and "sententious," presented by Puttenham, there are certain ones, a rather large number if all subdivisions of the main types are counted, which would seem to be fundamental to the logic of the formally ordered

"Rhetoric and Poems: Alexander Pope" by William Kurtz Wimsatt, Jr. From The Verbal Icon: Studies in the Meaning of Poetry (*Lexington: University of Kentucky Press, 1954*). *Copyright 1954 by University of Kentucky Press. Reprinted by permission of the publisher.*

verbal style. Thus, *"Parison,* or the figure of even [clauses]," *"Omoio-teleton,* or the figure of like-loose [like endings]," and *"Anaphora,* or the figure of report" (that is, repetition of a word at the beginning of successive clauses) are the figures in Puttenham which refer to formal parallels and which under one set of terms or another are a constant part of the rhetorical tradition from Puttenham back to Aristotle. Contrast or antithesis is the natural accompaniment of parallel. This appears in Puttenham as *"Antitheton,* or the quarreller, otherwise called the overthwart or rencounter." Wherever there is a parallel, there is a distinction, and wherever a distinction, the possibility of a paradox, an antithesis, or at least a modulation. Thus, to illustrate now from the verse of Pope:

> Who sees with equal eye, as God of all,
> A hero perish, or a sparrow fall.

> Favours to none, to all she smiles extends;
> Oft she rejects, but never once offends.

> Survey the WHOLE, nor seek slight faults to find
> Where nature moves, and rapture warms the mind.

This brings us, still quite naturally, to a third group of figures, those distinguished by Puttenham as *"Zeugma,* or the single supply" and *"Sillepsis,* or the double supply." Zeugma is further distinguished by Puttenham into *Prozeugma* (or the Ringleader), *Mezozeugma* (or the Middlemarcher), and *Hypozeugma* (or the Rerewarder), accordingly as the zeugma, or yoking word, occurs at the beginning, the middle, or the end of a total construction. He treats zeugma among the figures "merely *auricular* in that they reach no furder than the eare," and among figures "that work by defect," that is, by the absence of "some little portion of speech." He does not say anything about the relation of zeugma to parallel. But we might observe that zeugma or ellipsis is almost the inevitable effect of a tightened and precise economy of parallel. If A, B, C and X, B, Z are presented, then A, B, C and X, Z is an easy result; or if A, B and X, B, then A, B and X—in the more usual case, the parallel of two elements. Thus, in Pope's verse:

> *Who* could not win the mistress, wooed the maid. (Prozeugma)

> And now a bubble *burst,* and now a world. (Mezozeugma)

> Where nature moves, and rapture warms the *mind.* (Hypozeugma)

And, to note a special and significant kind of zeugma that occurs in Pope's verse, such examples as these:

> Or lose her heart, or necklace, at a ball.

> Or stain her honour or her new brocade.

This is metaphor. I mention it here not simply to list the figure of metaphor among Pope's accomplishments. Puttenham also duly lists *"Metaphora,* or the figure of transport." But here it seems to me curious, and worth noting, though it is not noted by Puttenham, that a series of several logical steps, distinction, parallel, then simplification or canceling a common element, has led us to metaphor, something that has often, and notably by some in Pope's day, been considered the very essence of the irrational or merely imaginative in poetry. Let us carry our series to its conclusion, returning to Puttenham for help. Consider the figure of *"Sillepsis,* or the double supply,"* which occurs according to Puttenham when a verb is used either with a double grammatical congruity, or in a double sense. The latter may be thus illustrated from Pope's verse.

> Here thou, great Anna! whom three realms obey,
> Dost sometimes counsel take—and sometimes tea.

> With earnest eyes, and round unthinking face,
> He first the snuff-box opened, then the case.

Worse and worse. We have now descended from logical parallel and ellipsis, through metaphor, into pun. In short, by starting with what might have been thought the most logical and prosaic aspects of Pope's verse (both *Antitheton* and *Parison* were mentioned by Puttenham as figures specially related to prose), and by moving through a few shades of meaning we have arrived at the very things which the modern critic Empson noticed first in looking for the shiftiness or ambiguity of this kind of verse. We may note too, as we pass, that the distinction between the two figures last described, the metaphoric zeugma and the punning syllepsis, is not always easy. Take the couplet preceding that about counsel and tea:

> Here Britain's statesmen oft the fall foredoom
> Of foreign Tyrants and of Nymphs at home.

It depends on how technically and specifically we are accustomed to think of a "fall" from virtue, whether we take "the fall of tyrants and of nymphs" as metaphor or pun.

Austin Warren

Zeugma, the joining of two unlike objects governed by a single verb,
is a form of pun; yet this verbal play constitutes one of Pope's most
poetic resources in the *Rape:* it is this device, one might say, which
gives the tone to the whole. Burlesque are both Pope's masterpieces,
the *Rape* and the *Dunciad.* Of the mock-epic, we may provisionally
say that it plays form against matter, a lofty and elaborate form
against a trivial situation or set of persons or theme. But "form against
matter" is too simple a naming. The real failure of the post-Miltonic
epic lay, surely, in the supposition that the heroic poem could be
written in an unheroic age; that a poem which, generically, involved
the interrelation of the human and the divine, the natural and the
supernatural, could be written in an age when "thinking people" had
grown too prudent for heroism, too sophisticated for religion. John
Dennis, whose taste among the Ancients was for Homer, Pindar, and
Sophocles, and among the Moderns for Milton, was not unsound in
his critical contention that great poetry like that of his favorites must
be religious. So we might restate the incongruity as between heroic
things and refined, between an age of faith and an age of reason. The
mock-epic reminds an unheroic age of its own nature: by historical
reference, it defines the "civilized" present.

Is Pope, then, satirizing Belinda's world? Yes, but lightly. His intent
is rather to juxtapose contrasting modes than to decide how far his
aristocracy has gained by its elegance, how far lost by its safe distance
from war, politics, poverty, and sin. The poem is in nothing more
dexterous than in its controlled juxtaposition of worlds. In another
context we should find ominous those brilliant lines which couple by
incongruity the worlds of the bourgeoisie and the proletariat with that
of the leisure class:

> The hungry Judges soon the sentence sign,
> And wretches hang that jury-men may dine;
> The merchant from the Exchange returns in peace,
> And the long labors of the Toilet cease.

"Alexander Pope" by Austin Warren. From Rage for Order *(Chicago: University
of Chicago Press, 1948). This article is a revision of "The Mask of Pope," Sewanee
Review, LIV (1946), 19–33. Copyright 1948 by University of Chicago Press. Reprinted by permission of the University of Chicago Press.*

The *Rape* owes its richness and resonance to its overstructure of powerful, dangerous motifs. What keeps it from being that filigree artifice which the romantics saw (and praised) is its playing with fire, especially the fires of sex and religion. Though Pope was scarcely a "good Catholic," his parents were devout; and he is writing of an "old Catholic" society; and many of his effects involve the suggestion of blasphemous parallels: the linking of English folklore and the Lives of the Saints, and of both to his gentle mythology of urbane "machines." He links the nurse's moonlit elves and fairy ring with the priest's tales of "virgins visited by Angel-powers"; the visions of the Cave of Spleen are

> Dreadful as hermit's dreams in haunted shades,
> Or bright as visions of expiring maids,

visions which may or may not be reducible to physiological disturbances; the Baron and Belinda have their altars to Pride and Love, their real religions.

What, for religion, is got by parody parallel is, for sexual morality, managed by insinuation. Though it is admitted that nymphs may break Diana's law, we see none do so; the titular *Rape* is but of a lock. The opening of Canto III (a preview for the *School for Scandal*) shows the chorus at work ("At every word a reputation dies"); but we do not hear the death. A characteristic passage of *double-entendre* retails the difficulty of preserving a "melting maid's" purity at such a time and place of temptation as the midnight masquerade, while assuring us that her male companions' Honor, or her sylph, preserves her virtue.

Without doubt the specific perspectives through parody and irony are purposed. But there may be doubt whether these effects are not local and episodic, unsubject to central design and all-governing tone; for, though silly things have been said about Pope's work of composition (as if "closed couplets" must all be equally discrete and unreconciled), he was, of course, so intent on making every verse exciting and finished as to make it difficult for the poem to subordinate them. In the case of the *Rape* he is often in danger but, I think, unvanquished. What organizes the poem is not exclusively the narrative, with its chronological and dramatic sequence of scenes (including two battles); it is yet more its tone—the steadiness with which it holds, against heroic and religious perspectives, to its seriocomic view of a little elegant society.

Not to the manor born, Pope makes the drawing-room seem an achievement. He so treats a woman's day, says Johnson, that "though nothing is disguised, everything is striking; and we feel all the appetite of curiosity for the form which we have a thousand times turned fastidiously away." Pope had not turned fastidiously away; like Proust, another "outsider," he was fascinated by the ritual which gave—or signified—the aristocratic status. He has practiced, on other matter, the Wordsworthian formula of giving to the unmarvelous the light of wonder. Society is a wonder, we are made to feel; convention a triumph of happy contrivance; coffee a luxury; a card game a crisis. This effect is in large measure the result of the "machinery" of sylphs, who not only contrast with Homer's and Milton's "machines" but parallel Pope's women—those coquettes, termagants, dociles, and prudes whose natures they abstract and stylize.

The burlesque of the *Rape* provides, then, an elaborate stratification of attitudes and effects: amusement at trifles taken seriously; delight at elegance; recollections of earlier literature (Homer and Spenser) in counterpoint against the current literary mode; juxtaposition of corresponding worlds (Achilles' shield, the great petticoat); reminders of the economic and political structures which make possible this leisure-class comedy, of the moral and religious structures which make possible a society at all.

Aubrey Williams

In *The Rape of the Lock* a most important pattern of imagery is established by pervasive reference to a wide variety of vessels: vases, bottles, pipkins, pots and China jars are signal and memorable articles of the poem's furniture. There is the array of jars on Belinda's dressing-table, the display of cups and silver pots on the sumptuous buffet, the collection of containers in the lunar limbo. . . . So much crockery in the poem can scarcely be ignored, and neither should the variety of special effects of Pope by its use. More particularly, awareness of the range of this vessel imagery serves to underscore its peculiar importance on three occasions when it relates most directly to the poem's central event.

*   *   *

The ultimate sources for all this vessel imagery seem undiscoverable: Freud, indeed, sees all imagery of containers to be feminine, and thus attributes archetypal status to it. Yet some possible ancient sources should be noted, principally the general Biblical tendency to

"*The 'Fall' of China and* The Rape of the Lock" *by Aubrey Williams. From* Philological Quarterly *XLI (1962), 412–25. Reprinted by permission of the author and publisher.*

use vessels as an image of man, and, more particularly, the passage in
1 Peter 3:7, which enjoins husbands to give "honour unto the wife,
as unto the weaker vessel." The stress of the injunction should be
observed: woman is accorded honor because she is the weaker vessel,
and so the passage suggests that the very fragility of the vessel, as of
feminine beauty and character in general, is somehow the source of the
value and honor accorded it. And alongside such Biblical usage, there
is the pagan classical tendency to see women as vessels. . . .

But regardless of the ultimate sources for such imagery, we can now
return to one of the crucial instances of its use in *The Rape of the
Lock,* these lines,

> Whether the Nymph shall break *Diana's* Law,
> Or some frail *China* Jar receive a Flaw,

and perhaps more easily describe some of its implications. The first
line of the couplet is relatively direct in its implications, and the
harshness of "break" is admirably set off against the more subdued
"receive" in the second line. This second line, on the other hand,
seems almost inexhaustible in its range of suggestions. First of all,
there is the suggestion, here as in much of the poem's vessel imagery,
that Pope is exploiting the Biblical image of woman as the weaker
vessel, and that he is in some sense doing homage to this vessel:
though Pope's view of her is laced with irony, Belinda's beauteous virginity is somehow rendered more precious, and our regard for it somehow more tender, by recognition of how easily it can be marred or
shattered. At the same time, Pope's "frail" and brittle China jar
humorously recalls the general view of women exemplified by Hamlet's exclamation, "Frailty, thy name is woman," or by George
Herbert's saying that "A woman and a glasse are ever in danger."
There is the hint of mortality inherent in all the imagery which likens
women to something so frangible as fine glass or China: existing in
a state of tremulous instability and inconstancy, the vessels seem to
lean of themselves towards disaster. Made of the dust and clay of
the earth, they seem destined for a shocking reversion to "glitt'ring
Dust and painted Fragments." Too, there are also all those inherent,
as well as inherited, suggestions of loss—loss of perfection, beauty and
virginity—so wittily engaged by the course of the poem and its central
event. All three of the poem's crucial images of the "fall" of China,
indeed, gather to themselves, and impart to the meaning of the poem
at large, all of these suggestions, along with one more. This is the suggestion, made with varying degrees of emphasis by the three images,

of the utter finality of the loss involved in the breaking of fine China,
or of the frail bond of chastity.

*   *   *

Given the world of Hampton Court, any attitude other than that
actually adopted by Belinda would have seemed to be a violation of
the poem's decorum. Yet it should also be recognized that, on the level
of the poem where the humor becomes a little stern and the examination of manners edges into an examination of morals, an opportunity
is given to Belinda to transcend the limitations of a world where
"honor" and "virtue" are equated with "reputation" and "appearance." Pope maintains the decorum of his poem, but this should not
obscure the fact that Belinda fails to meet the test of her spirit pro-
posed by Clarissa. Of course, as many critics have stressed, Pope's
attitude toward Belinda is very mixed and complicated: mocking and
yet tender, admiring and yet critical. This mixed and complicated
attitude, however, is at least partly the product of Pope's concern with
a "type" of human experience which simultaneously involves both
loss and gain, one in which loss must be suffered if the gain is to be at
all achieved. The paradoxical nature of Pope's attitude is thus inti-
mately related to the paradox of Belinda's situation, and to the
sexual terms of that situation: if Belinda is to find her role of woman,
she must lose the role of virgin, and the more graceful her acceptance
of loss the greater victory she achieves through it. Because Pope is
dealing with this paradox, his attitude must be mixed and complicated. He can appreciate virginal perfection, however narcissistic, and
"mourn" its loss; yet he can also give final honor to a kind of perfection achieved on another level. The loss of perfection and the marring
of beauty, imaged by the fall and shattering of rich China vessels, is
seen in the poem as an inevitable part of human experience. But in
recompence for her particular losses, Belinda is offered the gain of
a different kind of beauty and perfection: the kind Sarpedon achieved
through simple generosity of spirit in the face of his loss, the kind
Adam and Eve were offered after their loss. . . . Blinded by a false
sense of shame and thinking only of reputation, Belinda can scarcely
be expected to transcend the values of her society, but this does not
mean that the reader, whatever his anxiety not to spoil the hilarious
mockery of the occasion, is to ignore the ignominy of her real defeat,
or the sadnesses of the poem at large. For amidst all the glitter and
gaiety and irony, amidst all the shimmering brightness and lightness
and sheer fun of the poem, there are insistent reminders of the shades
just beneath and beyond the pale of paint and light.

Martin Price

In *The Rape of the Lock* we move from the nature-become-art of
the pastoral to the heroic-turned-artful. The world of Belinda is a
world of triviality measured against the epic scale; it is also a world of
grace and delicacy, a second-best world but not at all a contemptible
one. Here Pope has built upon a theme that plays against the epic
tradition: the mock-heroic world (in Dryden's version) of Virgil's bees
is a world that has some real, if extravagant, claim to the epic style.
The *Georgics* celebrate a mundane heroism and place it against the
special virtues of the martial hero.

The emphasis of the epic had, moreover, moved by Pope's day—
through Spenser and Milton—further and further toward spiritual
conflict. In *The Rape of the Lock* the primary quality of Belinda is
spiritual shallowness, an incapacity for moral awareness. She has
transformed all spiritual exercises and emblems into a coquette's
self-display and self-adoration. All of it is done with a frivolous heed-
lessness; she is not quite a hypocrite.

> Fair nymphs, and well-drest youths around her shone,
> But ev'ry eye was fix'd on her alone.
> On her white breast a sparkling cross she wore,
> Which Jews might kiss, and Infidels adore (II, 5–8).

Our perspective closes more and more sharply, upon Belinda as cyno-
sure, and upon the sparkling cross that fixes attention upon her
beauty. The cross is a religious symbol turned to the uses of ornament,
and by the rules of the little world of the poem it gains new power
through this translation. At every point in the poem grace and charm
supplant depth of feeling or heroic action; the only direct survivors
of the old heroic virtues are the miniature playing cards. Here Pope's
play with scale becomes most fascinating. Within the heroic frame
of the mock-epic language we have the miniature world of belles and
beaux, who live by an elaborate and formal set of rules. Within that
small world is framed in turn the card game (with its further formal-
ization of rules), where kings and queens, mortal battles and shameful seductions, still survive, as a game within a game.

From To The Palace of Wisdom: Studies in Order and Energy from Dryden to
Blake *by Martin Price. (New York, Doubleday & Company, Inc., 1964). Copyright
Martin Price, 1964. Reprinted by permission of Doubleday & Company, Inc.*

The principal symbol of the triviality of Belinda's world is the machinery of sylphs and gnomes. The "light militia of the lower sky" are a travesty of both Homeric deities and Miltonic guardian angels. Like their originals, they have an ambiguous status: they exist within and without the characters. They are, in their diminutive operation, like those small but constant self-regarding gestures we may associate with a lady conscious of her charms. The sylphs who protect Belinda are also her acceptance of the rules of social convention, which presume that a coquette's life is pure game. The central action of the poem is Belinda's descent from coquette to prude, from the dazzling rival of the sun ("Belinda smil'd, and all the world was gay") to the rancorous Amazon who shrieks in self-righteous anger. It is Clarissa who vainly points to the loss. Her speech in the last canto is a parody, as Pope reminds us, of Sarpedon's speech to Glaucus in Book XII of the *Iliad*. For "the utter generosity of spirit, the supreme magnanimity of attitude" with which Sarpedon faces the loss of life, Clarissa offers to Belinda a substitute that is analogous: within the scale of the playground world of the coquette there is the selflessness of "good humor," the ability to place value rightly and accept the conditions of life. This will permit Belinda to retain the radiance that has warmed and illumined her world.

Pope's use of scale has set up a double view of this play-world. It has the smallness of scale and fineness of organization of the work of art, yet like a game, it is temporary and threatens to break down. "At any moment 'ordinary life' may reassert its rights either by an impact from without, which interrupts the game, or by an offense against the rules, or else from within, by a collapse of the play spirit, a sobering, a disenchantment" (Huizinga, p. 21).* Clarissa's speech offers a view of life as it must be when the playing has to stop. Thalestris offers the outrage of the spoilsport. "By withdrawing from the game [the spoilsport] reveals the relativity and fragility of the play-world in which he had temporarily shut himself with others. He robs play of its *illusion*—a pregnant word which means literally 'in-play' (from *inlusio, illudere,* or *inludere*)" (Huizinga, p. 11).* Pope's play-world in *The Rape of the Lock* hovers between the trivial fragility of mere play (with its obliviousness to the possibilities of mature life) and the preciousness of a life ordered with grace, however minute its scale or limited its values.

In the dressing-table scene at the close of Canto I we see Belinda's beauty both as mere ornamentation governed by pride and as the realization of a genuine aesthetic ordering. The worship before the

* *Homo Ludens: A Study of the Play Element in Culture* (Boston, 1955)—*Ed.*

mirror of the "cosmetic powers" produces the appearance Belinda
wishes to have and which she further adorns, her maid attending "the
sacred Rites of Pride." With that word, the world pours in, diminished
in scale:

> Unnumber'd treasures ope at once, and here
> The various off'rings of the world appear. . . .
> This casket India's glowing gems unlocks,
> And all Arabia breathes from yonder box.
> The tortoise here and elephant unite,
> Transform'd to combs, the speckled and the white (129–30; 133–36).

The spacious world can enter Belinda's dressing room only in a
serviceable and diminished form. Arabia is compressed into its per-
fume; the unwieldy elephant and tortoise are transformed into the
elegance of shell and ivory combs. The universe, the Indian philosopher tells us, is a great elephant standing on the back of a tortoise.
John Locke had made much of the fable in his treatment of substance
(*Essay of Human Understanding*, II, ch. 23, para. 2). This condensa-
tion of the vast into the small is at once reversed: the pins extend into
"shining rows" or "files" of soldiers, and Belinda becomes the epic hero
investing himself in armor as well as the godlike "awful Beauty." Here
is the triumph of art: Belinda "calls forth all the wonders of her face"
and gives them realization with her cosmetic skill. She is the mistress
of the "bidden blush" but also the culmination of nature. Her art
trembles on the precipice of mere artifice, but it retains its poise.

We can say, then, that the world of Belinda is once more a pastoral
world, the world of the "town-eclogue." But it is filled with omens:
balanced against Belinda's rites of pride are the Baron's prayers at
another altar; balanced against Belinda's generous smiles are the
labyrinths of her hair. As she descends the Thames, the "painted
vessel" is the literal craft on which she sails and also Belinda herself—
perhaps reminiscent of the "stately Ship / Of Tarsus . . . With all
her bravery on, and tackle trim, / Sails filled, and streamers waving, /
Courted by all the winds that hold them play"—the Dalila of Milton's
Samson Agonistes. Belinda is at once the pastoral mistress ("Where'er
you walk, cool gales shall fan the glade"), the power of harmony, and
the imminent temptress and sower of discord. But her greatest power
arises from the fact that she is not really aware of what she is leading
the Baron to do or of what disaster may befall herself. Like Eve's, her
very weakness increases her power for destruction, and the sylphs,
lovely but variable, express her ambiguous self-consciousness—the
sense of disaster that is also a sense of her power to call forth violence.

Marjorie Hope Nicolson and G. S. Rousseau

No poet as late as Pope's generation needed technical training to teach him to coin figures from the very small in Nature. Perhaps some of Pope's persistent interest in "the poetry of little things" went back, in part at least, to his own smallness. He wrote his friend John Caryll on January 25, 1711, early in their correspondence:

'Tis certain the greatest magnifying glasses in the world are a mans own eyes, when they look upon his own person; yet even in those, I appear not the great Alexander Mr Caryll is so civil to, but that little Alexander the women laugh at.

Many years later he wrote in the *Epistle to Cobham* (11, 15–16):

> There's some Peculiar in each leaf and grain,
> Some unmark'd fibre, or some varying vein.

But Pope's eyesight was such that he could rarely have detected for himself minute peculiarities in leaf or grain. Rather, he drew many of his reiterated figures for the small from traditions, familiar from the author of Proverbs down to Sir Thomas Browne, which said in effect: "What Reason may not go to school to the wisdom of Bees, Ants, and Spiders?" Pope's many insect-references are largely non-microscopical. The earliest in "Phryne" had to do with one of the seeming miracles of Nature that has always fascinated human beings, insect metamorphosis:

> So have I known those Insects fair,
> (Which curious *Germans* hold so rare,)
>   Still vary Shapes and Dyes;
> Still gain new Titles with new Forms;
> First Grubs obscene, then wriggling Worms,
>   Then painted Butterflies.

Lines on "equivocal generation" in *An Essay on Criticism* go back at least as far as Ovid:

> Those half-learn'd Witlings, num'rous in our Isle,
> As half-form'd Insects on the Banks of *Nile*;

> Unfinish'd Things, one knows not what to call,
> Their Generation's so *equivocal*.

Read in their context, these lines too—with the double-play of meaning in "equivocal"—deal with metamorphosis, though devolutionary
rather than evolutionary. They occur in a verse-paragraph beginning:

> Some have at first for *Wits*, then *Poets* past,
> Turn'd *Criticks* next, and prov'd plain *Fools* at last.

The same idea is implied in *To a Lady*:

> So morning Insects that in muck begun,
> Shine, buzz, and fly-blow in the setting-sun.

Few minor motifs are more reiterative in Pope's writing at various
periods of his life than insects and maggots. He wrote to Caryll on
August 14, 1713: "Who knows what plots, what achievements a mite
may perform, in his kingdom of a grain of dust, within his life of some
minutes?" Complaining of the hot weather, he wrote Arbuthnot on
July 11, 1714: "This is not a Time for us to make others live, when
we can hardly live ourselves; so Scriblerus (contrary to other Maggotts)
must lye dead all the Summer, & wait till Winter shall revive him."
Ironically enough, he used the figure, with very different undertones,
in a letter to Hugh Bethel, February 20, 1744, three months before his
death: "I live like an Insect, in hope of reviving with the Spring."
    Deft as he was, Pope could play upon this theme in many moods,
laughing, satiric, serious. He overdid the figure in an early minor
poem, "To Mr. John Moore," though he doubtless justified the exaggeration by his subtitle, "Author of the Celebrated Worm-Powder,"
since Moore was a notorious quack. Book-worms, glow-worms, slow-
worms, muck-worms, silk-worms—they are all here in profusion. Particularly:

> Man is a very Worm by Birth,
>   Vile Reptile, weak, and vain!
> A while he crawls upon the Earth,
>   Then shrinks to Earth again. . . .
> The Fops are painted Butterflies,
>   That Flutter for a Day;
> First from a Worm they take their Rise,
>   And in a Worm decay.

In his major works, however, Pope handles the many insect-figures
deftly and usually succinctly. Sometimes they emphasize the ephemeral:

> Ye tinsel Insects! whom a Court maintains,
> That counts your Beauties only by your Stains,
> Spin all your Cobwebs o'er the Eye of Day!
> The Muse's wing shall brush you all away.

In an extended passage in *Dunciad I* upon stylistic matters, poems and plays emerge from an original Chaos, "Hints, like spawn, scarce quick in embryo lie," whimsical fancies like

> Maggots half form'd, in rhyme exactly meet,
> And learn to crawl upon poetic feet.

Largely Pope used insect-figures to stress insignificance, particularly in man. In one instance in the *Epistle to Burlington* memories of the relativity of small and great seem to have hovered in Pope's mind from *Gulliver's Travels.* The specious magnificence of Timon's Villa is introduced:

> Greatness, with Timon, dwells in such a draught
> As brings old Brobdingnag before your thought.

The true insignificance of the villa-owner is emphasized by an insect-figure:

> Who but must laugh, the Master when he sees,
> A puny insect, shiv'ring at a breeze!

This couplet was wickedly rewritten by Lady Mary Wortley Montagu and Lord Hervey to describe Pope himself:

> Who but must laugh, this Bully when he sees,
> A little Insect shiv'ring at a Breeze?

Lines on the small, familiar to most readers from *An Epistle to Dr. Arbuthnot,* were first published in 1727 in "A Fragment of a Satire":

> Pretty, in Amber to observe the forms
> Of Hairs, or Straws, or Dirt, or Grubs, or Worms:
> The *Thing,* we know, is neither rich nor rare,
> But wonder how the Devil it got there.

Based upon a poem by William Dingley, "Upon a Bee Entom'd in Amber," this quatrain follows still another classical tradition. A somewhat similar amber-figure had been used by Tacitus in the *Germania,* and Pliny in the *Natural History,* but Dingley's source— and hence Pope's—was Martial, *Epigrams* IV, 32, a common schoolboy exercise throughout the seventeenth century.

No reader of Pope needs to be reminded of his most exquisite

adaptation of the small in the Rosicrucian "machinery" of the revised
Rape of the Lock, with the "Denizens of Air," summoned by the
Sylph:

> Transparent Forms, too fine for mortal Sight,
> Their fluid Bodies half dissolv'd in Light.

Their minuteness is seen in the passage on punishments designed for
those who broke the rules, who should

> Be stopt in *Vials,* or transfixt with *Pins,*
> Or plung'd in Lakes of bitter *Washes* lie,
> Or wedg'd whole Ages in a *Bodkin's* Eye. . . .
> Or Alom-*Stypticks* with contracting Power
> Shrink his thin Essence like a rivell'd Flower.

Pope did, however, introduce microscopical figures into both his
prose and his poetry, although these too came to him less from personal observation than from literary tradition. Again, it is probable
that Pope's eye problems made it difficult if not impossible for him
to observe at first hand as did many of his immediate predecessors
and contemporaries. It is significant that on the one occasion on which
he referred to a real instrument it was his mother rather than Pope
himself who made the observation. Writing to John Caryll on February 18, 1718, he mentioned a "seasonable acquaintance" with "Mr.
Hatton," a clockmaker, who "is likewise curious in microscopes and
showed my mother some of the *semen masculinum* with animascula in
it." Pope's most charming microscopical adaptations appear in "Verses
on *Gulliver's Travels,*" written in Scriblerian mood, and published by
Swift in the second edition. In "The Words of the King of Brobding-
nag, As he held Captain Gulliver between his Finger and Thumb,"
Pope followed in the train of various writers of the late seventeenth
century when the microscopical fad was at its height.

> In Miniature see *Nature's* Power appear;
> Which wings the Sun-born Insects of the Air,
> Which frames the Harvest-bug, too small for Sight,
> And forms the Bones and Muscles of the Mite!
> Here view him stretch'd. The Microscope explains,
> That the Blood, circling, flows in human Veins;
> See, in the Tube he pants, and sprawling lies,
> Stretches his little Hands, and rolls his Eyes.

The "Sun-born Insects of the Air" momentarily recall the passage in
The Rape of the Lock, in which the sylphids "to the Sun their Insect-

Wings unfold." Like many others, Pope not only recalls various insects, "too small for human sight," but is aware that seventeenth-century microscopists had demonstrated the circulation of blood in mites as well as in men—and Gulliver here is both man and mite.

Chronology of Important Dates

	Pope	The Age
1688	Alexander Pope born in London of elderly parents (May 21).	The "Glorious Revolution," which displaced the Stuart James II with the Dutch William III.
1689		William III ascends the throne; William and Mary reign (1689–1702).
1700	Pope's family moved to Binfield, in Windsor Forest.	Death of Dryden. Congreve's *Way of the World.*
1702		Reign of Queen Anne, James II's daughter (1702–14). Beginning of the War of the Spanish Succession (1702–13).
1704		Battle of Blenheim. Capture of Gibraltar. Swift's *Tale of a Tub.*
1705	Acquaintance with the "Wits," the literary society of London.	
1707		Union of England and Scotland.
1710		Fall of the Whigs. Tory government under Harley and Bolingbroke.
1711	*An Essay on Criticism* published.	Addison and Steele's *Spectator* (1711–12). Marlborough dismissed.
1712	Lintot's *Miscellany* published, containing the first version of *The Rape of the Lock.*	

1713	Pope studies painting with Jervas. *Windsor Forest* published.	Treaty of Utrecht.
1714	The enlarged version of *The Rape of the Lock*.	Death of Queen Anne. Whig government and House of Hanover under King George I (1714–27).
1715		First Jacobite rebellion, i.e., effort to restore the Stuarts to the English throne.
1720		South Sea Bubble.
1721	*The Epistle to Addison* published.	Robert Walpole prime minister (1721–42).
1728	*The Dunciad* published in three books.	Reign of George II (1727–60) and Queen Caroline.
1729	*The Variorum Dunciad* (with notes).	
1733	*An Essay on Man* (i–iii), the first. *Imitation of Horace, Epistle to Bathurst* published.	
1735	*Epistle to Dr. Arbuthnot* published.	
1737	Pope's edition of his letters. Pope's *Epistle to Augustus* (i.e., George II).	Death of Queen Caroline. Licensing Act.
1741		War of the Austrian Succession (1741–48).
1742	*The New Dunciad* (an early version of Book IV).	
1743	*The Dunciad* published in four books.	
1744	Death of Pope (May 30).	
1745		Death of Swift.

Notes on the Editor and Contributors

G. S. ROUSSEAU, the editor of this volume, teaches English literature at the University of California, Los Angeles. He is the author of numerous articles about Pope and a study (written with Marjorie Hope Nicolson) entitled *This Long Disease, My Life: Alexander Pope and the Sciences*.

LAWRENCE BABB is Professor of English at Michigan State University and the author of *Sanity in Bedlam: A Study of Robert Burton's Anatomy of Melancholy*.

CLEANTH BROOKS, Professor of English at Yale University, is the author of numerous books: *Understanding Poetry, The Language of Poetry, The Well Wrought Urn*.

REUBEN A. BROWER is Professor of English at Harvard University. His books include studies of Shakespeare, Dryden, and Robert Frost. He is also the author of *Alexander Pope: The Poetry of Allusion*.

J. S. CUNNINGHAM is a Senior Lecturer in English at the University of York and the author of the Introduction to *Pope: The Rape of the Lock*.

WILLIAM EMPSON is a well-known English poet and critic. Among his critical works are *Seven Types of Ambiguity, Some Versions of Pastoral* and *The Structure of Complex Words*.

WILLIAM FROST, Professor of English at the University of California, Santa Barbara, has written on Chaucer, Shakespeare, and Dryden, and on Pope and the classical tradition. He contributed to the Twickenham edition of Pope's translations of Homer.

IAN JACK is University Lecturer in English Literature at Pembroke College, Cambridge University and the author of *Augustan Satire*, a study of English burlesque poetry.

MARJORIE HOPE NICOLSON is a member of the Institute for Advanced Study at Princeton. She has written many books including *Newton Demands the Muse, Science and Imagination*, and *Mountain Gloom and Mountain Glory*.

REBECCA P. PARKIN, Assistant Professor of English at Sacramento State College, is the author of *The Poetic Workmanship of Alexander Pope*.

MARTIN PRICE, Professor of English at Yale University, has written extensively on Swift, Pope, and Dickens, and is the co-author of *English Prose and Poetry 1660–1800.*

AUSTIN WARREN was influential in promoting the New Criticism in the United States. His essays have been collected in *Rage for Order;* he also wrote *Alexander Pope as Critic and Humanist.*

EARL WASSERMAN is Professor of English at the Johns Hopkins University. Among his books are *The Finer Tone: Keats' Major Poems, The Subtler Language: Critical Readings of Neoclassic and Romantic Poems,* and *Pope's Epistle to Bathurst.*

AUBREY WILLIAMS is Professor of English at the University of Florida. He has written several books, including *Pope's Dunciad,* and edited Pope's *Pastoral Poetry* and *An Essay on Criticism* for the Twickenham series.

WILLIAM KURTZ WIMSATT, JR. is Professor of English at Yale University and the author of many books dealing with theory of criticism and with Pope and the eighteenth century. Among them are *The Verbal Icon, Hateful Contraries,* and *The Portraits of Alexander Pope.*

Selected Bibliography

Adler, Jacob H. *The Reach of Art: A Study in the Prosody of Alexander Pope.* Gainesville: University of Florida Press, 1964. Discusses Pope's use of meter, verse form, and other aspects of prosody.

Auden, W. H. "Alexander Pope," *Essays in Criticism*, Vol. I (1951).

Bond, Richmond P. *English Burlesque Poetry 1700–1750.* Cambridge, Mass.: Harvard University Press, 1932. Detailed and authoritative study of burlesque poetry in the Augustan age.

Edwards, Thomas R., Jr. *This Dark Estate: A Reading of Pope.* Berkeley: University of California Press, 1963. A critical interpretation of the poetry of Pope.

Hyman, Stanley Edgar. "The Rape of the Lock." *Hudson Review*, XIII (1960), 406–12. An eccentric but provocative essay describing the poem as "one vast comic defloration."

Jackson, James L. "Pope's *The Rape of the Lock* considered as a five-act epic." *Publications of the Modern Language Association*, LXV (1950), 1283–87. Pope relied on the conventional five-part dramatic structure of the Elizabethans and their successors for his organization of his much expanded mock-epic.

Mack, Maynard. *Essential Articles for the Study of Alexander Pope.* Hamden, Conn.: Archon Books; 1964.

———. " 'Wit and Poetry and Pope.' " In *Pope and His Contemporaries: Essays Presented to George Sherburn,* ed. James L. Clifford and Louis A. Landa, Oxford: Clarendon Press, 1949, pp. 20–40.

———. "The Muse of Satire." *Yale Review* (1951), pp. 80–92. Show how Pope's satiric persona affects qualities of the hero, the ingenue, and the *vir bonus* to achieve comic ends.

Martin, L. C. "Lucretius and *The Rape of the Lock*," *Review of English Studies,* XX (1944), 299–303. Parallels between Pope's poem and *De Rerum Natura.*

Nicolson, Marjorie and Rousseau, G. S. *This Long Disease, My Life: Alexander Pope and the Sciences.* Princeton: Princeton University Press, 1968. Microscopic and telescopic discovery influenced Pope's sylph machinery.

Tillotson, Geoffrey. *On the Poetry of Pope.* New York: Oxford University Press, 1938. Pope's poetry in the light of his culture and the ideas prevailing in his time.

————, ed. *The Rape of the Lock: The Twickenham Edition.* London: Methuen & Co., Ltd., 1962. Definitive annotated edition of the poem.

Wimsatt, W. K., Jr. "The Game of Ombre in *The Rape of the Lock.*" *Review of English Studies,* New Series (April 1950), pp. 136–43. Summarizes and adds to the arguments that appeared in the *Times Literary Supplement.*

TWENTIETH CENTURY
INTERPRETATIONS

MAYNARD MACK, *Series Editor*
Yale University

NOW AVAILABLE
Collections of Critical Essays
ON

ADVENTURES OF HUCKLEBERRY FINN
ALL FOR LOVE
THE AMBASSADORS
ARROWSMITH
AS YOU LIKE IT
BLEAK HOUSE
THE BOOK OF JOB
THE CASTLE
DOCTOR FAUSTUS
DUBLINERS
THE DUCHESS OF MALFI
EURIPIDES' ALCESTIS
THE FALL OF THE HOUSE OF USHER
THE FROGS
GRAY'S ELEGY
THE GREAT GATSBY
GULLIVER'S TRAVELS
HAMLET
HARD TIMES
HENRY IV, PART TWO
HENRY V
THE ICEMAN COMETH
JULIUS CAESAR

(continued on next page)

(continued from previous page)